Starting In Stocks

Rowland Webb

Visit our website at www.TheOrdinaryInvestor.com

Book design by Rowland Webb Jr.

ISBN-13: 9781797613673

DEDICATION

This workbook is dedicated to my wife, Erica, my three daughters Alexis, Olivia, and Lauren, my friends, and all of those who are trying to figure out how to create wealth for themselves and their families.

CONTENTS

CHAPTER 1: WHAT IS A STOCK?

Stock is a stake in a company. Large companies decide to go public in order to get investment from the public. In owning the stock in a particular company, you are able to participate in the growth of that company. For individuals, stock ownership gives you the ability to participate in the voting that goes on in the company along with distributions from the company called dividends. An individual or "retail investor" normally gains access to the stock identified as "Common Stock." This is the stock that is acquired through your brokerage firm, the company that you must go through in order to buy and sell shares of stock.

In general, we hear terms like: Market Cap, Large Cap, Mid Cap, Small Cap, Growth Stocks, Income Stocks, and Value Stocks. In summary, market capitalization is the total perceived value of a company, the "Cap" size is the category in which a particular company fits. The companies valued over ten billion dollars are categorized as large cap stocks, companies valued below two billion dollars are categorized as small cap stocks, and those companies between two and ten billion dollars in value are categorized as mid cap stocks. Growth stocks typically have company earnings growing at a faster rate than the market average and have a tendency not to distribute dividend payments, income stocks tend to distribute dividend payments regularly, and value stocks are stocks that seem to be underpriced at the moment due to having a lower price-to-earnings (PE) ratio than normal.

Stock Categories

Common stock is the kind most investors buy. Common stock generally gives one vote at shareholder meetings for every share owned. Common stock holders may also be entitled to receive distributions of the companies provides, called "dividend payments."

Preferred stock generally does not have voting rights, and you generally will not find them trading on an exchange. However, preferred stock shares have the benefit of "preference" for dividend payments; if a company decides it is going to pay dividends, preferred stock holders may get a bigger share, and be paid before common stock holders. Preferred stock holders are also entitled to be paid first if a company goes bankrupt and all the assets are sold off.

Common

Preferred

Stock Categories

Market Cap
total value or size of company

Large Cap
10 billion +

(mega 200 billion +)

Mid Cap
2 billion-10 billion

Small Cap
less than 2 billion

(micro: 2 billion- 50 million, nano: less than 50 million)

Growth
Growth stocks have earnings growing at a faster rate than the market average. They rarely pay dividends and investors buy them in the hope of capital appreciation. A start-up technology company is likely to be a growth stock.

Income
Income stocks pay dividends consistently. Investors buy them for the income they generate. An established utility company is likely to be an income stock..

Value
Value stocks have a low price-to-earnings (PE) ratio, meaning they are cheaper to buy than stocks with a higher PE. Value stocks may be growth or income stocks, and their low PE ratio may reflect the fact that they have fallen out of favor with investors for some reason. People buy value stocks in the hope that the market has overreacted and that the stock's price will rebound.

CHAPTER 2: WHY SHOULD I INVEST IN STOCKS?

Investing in stocks is a personal choice. Many statistics have highlighted that those individuals who are not investing are missing out on the opportunity to gain significant yearly returns on their money and participate in the wealth creation that happens in the United States. If you notice the trends in who carries a majority of wealth in this country, you will find that many of them own shares of stock in various companies. As a matter of fact, the individuals who fluctuate at the top of the wealth lists do so in part to the increase in value of their particular stock holdings. Is it a coincidence that top company executives own shares of their company as part of the compensation package as opposed to just getting more money? There is something to be said about the growth potential that lies within partial ownership of a company.

There are several reasons to invest in stocks: the stock market has proven to be a vehicle that has created wealth over time, participation in the stock market has proven to be a great hedge against inflation (or the rising cost of goods and services), involvement in the stock market helps individuals to be on the right side of financial statistics, participation in the stock market provides numerous ways to be able to invest money for growth opportunities, the stock market provides a vehicle for an individual to take advantage of compound interest, you do not need large sums of money to start participating in buying stocks, and company stock purchases allow the individual to participate in a company's earnings in a passive capacity. This workbook will examine different statistics to help you formulate your own conclusions on the validity of these reasons.

Why Should I Invest In Stocks?

The stock market has proven to be a great vehicle to create wealth over time.

To hedge against inflation

To be on the right side of the financial statistics

You can invest in different ways

To take advantage of the effects of compound interest

Does not take large investment to get started

Ownership

The stock market has proven to be a great vehicle to accumulate wealth over time. It has been said that the stock market is one of the crucial components to wealth creation. I have provided several time frames for you to compare of the stock market bench mark, the S&P 500. With these charts, you can examine the movement of the S&P 500 over the periods of one year, five years, and twenty five years to give some long and short term examples of recent growth. Please keep in mind that the S&P 500 (Standard & Poor's 500 Index) is a combination of between five hundred to five hundred and five of the largest U.S. companies in various categories (sectors). The companies that come in and out of this index vary over time to keep the strongest companies in and release those companies that that have fallen out of the top spots in terms of market value. Also, keep in mind that individual company stocks can move at higher or lower rates compared to the S&P 500 index.

The stock market has proven to be a great vehicle to create wealth over time.

Open 273.45
High 275.85
Low 263.31
Close 263.93
Volume 294.68 M
% Change 4.18%

SPDR S&P 500 ETF
270.06 +0.13 (+0.06%)
At close February 1, 4:00 PM EST

1 year chart
Feb 4, 2018- Feb 1, 2019

The stock market has proven to be a great vehicle to create wealth over time.

Open	177.97
High	179.87
Low	173.71
Close	179.68
Volume 887.74 M	
% Change 0.64%	

SPDR S&P 500 ETF
270.06 +0.13 (+0.06%)
At close February 1, 4:00 PM EST

5 year chart
Feb 3, 2014- Feb 1, 2019

The stock market has proven to be a great vehicle to create wealth over time.

Open   46.84
High   47.44
Low   46.81
Close   46.97
Volume 2.25 M
% Change 7.33%

SPDR S&P 500 ETF
270.06 +0.13 (+0.06%)
At close February 1, 4:00 PM EST

25 year chart
Feb 3, 1994- Feb 1, 2019

The stock market has proven to be a great hedge against inflation or the rising cost of goods and services over time. Examples are used from an inflation calculator and an average cost of goods list to demonstrate that the cost of goods has indeed gone up over time. While having several conversations with my parents and grandparents, I have been able to get a grip on how drastic the changes have been. They can recall things that I had never had the chance to experience such a "penny candy" and loaves of bread and coke products that they were able to purchase for a nickel. You can also get a quick lesson by asking how much their first car purchase was.

As you do research about the development of the United States economy, you will start to see hints of the value of a dollar declining over time and how it is designed to get weaker and weaker over time. While saving is a critical and valuable skill to have, we must invest our money so that it keeps up with the times.

To hedge against inflation

How much a dollar back then would be worth in 2018

(based on an Inflation Calculator)

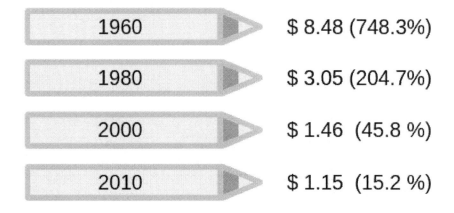

| 1960 | $ 8.48 (748.3%) |

| 1980 | $ 3.05 (204.7%) |

| 2000 | $ 1.46 (45.8 %) |

| 2010 | $ 1.15 (15.2 %) |

Year	Average Wages	Average Cost of New Home	Average Cost of New Car	Average cost of gallon of gas	Average cost of a loaf of bread	Average cost of 1lb of hamburger meat
1930	$1,970	$3,845	$600	$0.10	$0.09	$0.12
1940	$1,725	$3,920	$850	$0.11	$0.10	$0.20
1950	$3,210	$8,450	$1,510	$0.18	$0.12	$0.30
1960	$5,315	$12,700	$2,600	$0.25	$0.22	$0.45
1970	$9,400	$23,450	$3,450	$0.36	$0.25	$0.70
1980	$19,500	$68,700	$7,200	$1.19	$0.50	$0.99
1990	$28,960	$123,000	$16,950	$1.34	$0.70	$0.89
2008/2009	$40,523	$238,880	$27,958	$2.05	$2.79	$3.99
2012/2013	$44,321	$289,500	$31,352	$3.80	$1.98	$4.68

There are several financial statistics out there that you could examine. Most of these statistics highlight the state of emergency that the average person or family has with their finances. While a lack of financial planning can lead to various life complications, it is critical that we examine the state of affairs for the average person. Most of the statistics glaringly point out that individuals need to increase their financial literacy so they can have better outcomes with money. Continuing on your journey to improve your financial literacy can assist in you leaving or avoiding the negative side of the financial statistics to joining the positive side of the financial statistics out there. While there are hundreds of stats to review, I have listed a few for you to analyze. While analyzing these statistics, be sure to think about what the statistics mean on a surface level and on a larger scale.

To be on the right side of the financial statistics

Negative

ONLY 39% OF AMERICANS HAVE ENOUGH EMERGENCY SAVINGS TO COVER A $500-$1,000 EMERGENCY

A REPORT IN TIME FINDS 1 IN 3 AMERICANS (33%) HAVE $0 SAVED FOR RETIREMENT.

29% OF HOUSEHOLDS 55 AND OVER HAVE NO RETIREMENT SAVINGS OR PENSION

75% LIVE PAYCHECK TO PAYCHECK AT LEAST SOME OF THE TIME; 25% DO IT ALL THE TIME

A Gallup poll found only about 1/3 of Americans (32%) maintain a household budget

Interestingly enough, low income is not always to blame for financial hardship. Only 1 in 5 people (20%) facing financial hardship fall below the poverty line and make less than $40,000 per year

Positive

A RECORD NUMBER OF PEOPLE BECAME "401(K) MILLIONAIRES" IN THE FIRST QUARTER OF 2018, ACCORDING TO FIDELITY. THIS MEANS THEIR BALANCE HAS HIT THAT MAGICAL MILLION-DOLLAR NUMBER.

The average FICO credit score broke records in 2017 – the average American has a 700 FICO score.

The stock market gives you the ability to invest in a variety of ways. While it can at times be overwhelming, you do have the freedom of choice and can choose the ways in which you wish to participate in the stock market. You can choose individual companies to invest in as well as baskets of companies called funds. The individual companies give you hundreds of companies to choose from and the funds also give you a variety of choices. You can invest in an index fund in which you can invest in large baskets of companies under one stock, which allows for instant diversification and a safety net that protects from big downturns if a few companies are not performing well. You can invest in target date funds that automatically adjust risk tolerance as you get closer to retirement age. You can invest in individual sectors (categories) such as technology, consumer discretionary, health care, or energy. In summary, there are plenty of ways in which you can participate if you choose to do so. You have the ultimate freedom to pick and choose your investments in terms that are as specific or as broad as you like them to be.

Sector ETFs

XLP	**Consumer Staples**
XLV	**Health Care**
XLRE	**Real Estate**
XLC	**Communication Services**
XLE	**Energy**
XLI	**Industrial**
XLK	**Technology**
XLY	**Consumer Discretionary**
XLB	**Materials**
XLF	**Financials**
XLU	**Utilities**

Sector ETF Examples

XLY
Consumer Discretionary

AMZN	Amazon.com Inc
HD	Home Depot Inc
MCD	McDonald's Corp
NKE	Nike Inc
BKNG	Booking Holdings Inc
SBUX	Starbucks Corp
LOW	Lowe's Cos Inc
TJX	TJX Cos Inc
GM	General Motors Company
TGT	Target Corp

XLK
Technology

MSFT	Microsoft Corp
AAPL	Apple Inc
V	Visa Inc
INTC	Intel Corp
CSCO	Cisco Systems Inc
MA	Mastercard Inc
ORCL	Oracle Corp
ADBE	Adobe Inc
IBM	Intl Business Machines Corp
CRM	Salesforce.com

Investing is a way to take advantage of compound interest. Compound interest is the notion that your money grows exponentially by interest being reinvested over time to gain more interest. Albert Einstein is often quoted saying, "Compound interest is the eighth wonder of the world." Even if you are gaining a small amount of interest, the gains can be quite massive with time and consistency. The theory of compound interest is the reason why people invest in growth and income stocks.

In the examples listed, you will notice differences in the length of investment time, rates of return, and the total dollar amounts invested. Analyze each scenario to see how the length of time invested and the yearly interest rate on the money impacts each outcome.

To take advantage of the effects of compound interest

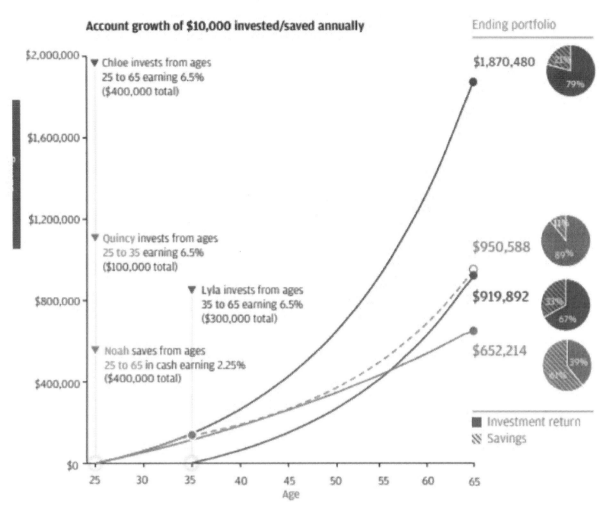

Account growth of $10,000 invested/saved annually

Ending portfolio

- ▼ Chloe invests from ages 25 to 65 earning 6.5% ($400,000 total)
- ▼ Quincy invests from ages 25 to 35 earning 6.5% ($100,000 total)
- ▼ Lyla invests from ages 35 to 65 earning 6.5% ($300,000 total)
- ▼ Noah saves from ages 25 to 65 in cash earning 2.25% ($400,000 total)

$1,870,480

$950,588

$919,892

$652,214

■ Investment return
≈ Savings

The above example is for illustrative purposes only and not indicative of any investment. Account value in this example assumes a 6.5% annual return an assumes a 2.25% annual return. Source: J.P. Morgan Asset Management, Long-Term Capital Market Assumptions. Compounding refers to the process of e return on principal plus the return that was earned earlier.

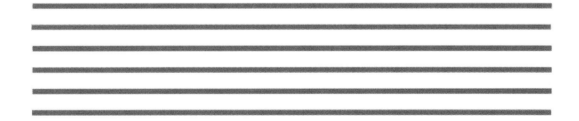

To take advantage of the effects of compound interest

Saving Steven saves $6,000 per year at 2.5% interest in a CD or Money Market Account until retirement. Halfway Harry invests $6,000 per year at 10% for his first ten working years, then stops investing. Late Start Lucy starts investing $6,000 per year at 10% after working for ten years until she retires. Diligent Dylan invests $6,000 per year at 10% from the time he starts work until the time he retires.

	10 years	20 years	30 years	40 years
Steven	$67,220	$153,268	$263,416	$404,415
Harry	$95,624	$248,026	$643,314	$1,668,591
Lucy	$0	$95,624	$343,650	$986,964
Dylan	$95,624	$343,650	$986,964	$2,655,555

Wealth after the years

It does not take a large amount of money to get started in the stock market. There are stocks that can be purchased from $1 all the way up to $2000+. Anyone that chooses to participate can open up a brokerage account or finance app and get started. There are also apps like Robinhood, Acorns, and Stockpile to help make it easier for individuals to start investing.

Ownership also has its advantages. Owning stock is like having a piece of a company that is doing the work for you. I tend to think of stock ownership as the opportunity for me to have hundreds and thousands of employees working to increase the value of my investment without having to do the majority of the work. Stock ownership can also come with regular company distributions called "dividends." In addition to growth in the stock, dividends can be reinvested to increase the impact of compound interest over time.

This is an example of how dividends work in an account. Some stocks give out a dividend (most times quarterly) for being a shareholder of a stock. This is an example of how ownership has benefits. The dividend amount is different for each company. Be cautious if dividends are extremely high and be sure to research the history (charts and news) of each company.

●●●○○ AT&T 📶   3:13 PM   ⏰ ⁎ 58% 🔋

✕   History   Filter

Pending

PG Dividend
Feb 15, 2019   +$4.30 >

T Dividend
Feb 1, 2019   +$17.85 >

VZ Dividend
Feb 1, 2019   +$1.21 >

FB Call Debit Spread
Jan 31, 2019   Placed >

FB 4-Option Order
Jan 31, 2019   Placed >

SPY Dividend
Jan 31, 2019   +$57.42 >

CHAPTER 3: WHAT SHOULD I INVEST IN?

This seems to be one of the hardest questions to answer even though it is probably one of the easiest. We are in the age of consumerism where everyone is using goods and services on a regular basis. To be honest, the answer lies within you. We are the perfect consumer. Companies spend millions of dollars per year trying to figure out how to get the consumers to purchase their product. Whether the reasonings are convenience, price, or service, one thing we can do is analyze our own habits and analyze our surrounding environment to find our answer.

I would like to challenge you to write down everything you do for three days to see what products and services you interact with on a daily basis. Peter Lynch, famous investor and mutual fund manager, often expresses that we have the keys to understanding what investments to make. It makes sense to invest in companies that we use and understand. If you thought about what products and services you use from the time you get up until the time you go to bed, you would be amazed. Look at a label and do some quick research to see how you can participate in companies that you already spend money on. You can start by asking yourself, "What did I do?," "What did I wear?," "What did I eat?," and "What did I use?"

You may also come to find that some products and services have been acquired by larger entities. To jog your memory, I have given you a few examples of some larger companies that have several brands within their company. Then, start to compile your own list. The chances are that if you use it, then someone else probably does as well.

 # What Stocks or Companies Should I Invest In ?

Think about ...

What you did?	
What you ate?	
What you wear?	
Things you use	
on a daily or	
weekly basis?	

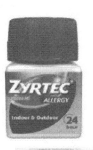
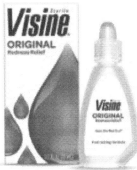

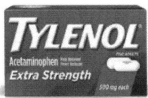

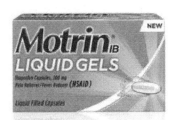

CHAPTER 4: WHAT ABOUT MY RETIREMENT AT WORK?

Many companies tend to offer some sort of retirement plan for their employees to participate in. Even if one is not available to you at work, you have the ability to set up retirement accounts with outside companies that offer retirement services. In using plans set up at work or on your own, it is prudent to carefully examine what your money is wrapped up in and how much you can contribute to these plans. This is probably the most important account you have as it is the one that is meant to sustain your standard of living after you retire (in most places pensions are long gone).

The first thing to consider is if the company is offering any match on your retirement contributions. If you can afford to do so, it is wise to invest at least the amount that the company matches. This is free money for you in those accounts. By matching your contribution, the company gives you a one hundred percent return on that portion. The second thing to look out for are the options that you are presented with. Some funds can charge a large portion of fees, that can eat up significant amounts of your investment returns.

I have included current contribution limitations from the IRS.gov website, an actual investment statement for you to analyze, and some fee statistics for your consideration. Please pay attention to the numbers very carefully as they tell a story all on their own.

How much can you contribute to your retirement plan?

IRA (Traditional/Roth)	$6,000 ($7,000 if age 50+)
401 K	cannot exceed $19,000
SEP IRA	lesser of $56,000 or 25% of compensation
SARSEPs	lesser of $19,000 or 25% of compensation
SIMPLE IRA	cannot exceed $13,000 or up to $19,000 with multiple plans
403(b)	cannot exceed $19,000 ($25,000 if age 50+)
457(b)	lesser of $19,000 or 100% of compensation

*Please consult the IRS.gov website for all details of each plan. This is for the year 2019

https://www.irs.gov/retirement-plans/plan-participant-employee/retirement-topics-ira-contribution-limits

Make sure you take your company match if it is offered, its free money.

If you have an average salary of $55,000 and your company matches up to 3% of your salary, how much free money could you leave on the table each year?

This is an actual statement with the different funds. Compare the expense ratios and percentage returns of the Vanguard 500 Index to the target date retirement funds.

Fund Number Investment Options	Gross / Net Fund Expense Ratio *	3-Mo	1-Yr	5-Yr	10-Yr/ Inception	Fu
Stability of Principal						
Money Market						
2574-BlackRock Liquidity Fed Trst Fd Inst	0.24%/0.17%	0.40%	1.17%	0.33%	0.29%	
The 7-day annualized yield as of 06/30/2018 is 1.73%, which more closely reflects current earnings. (1)						
Stability of Principal						
4020-Voya Fixed Plus Account III		0.43%	1.75%	2.00%	2.43%	
Bonds						
Inflation-Protected Bond						
1035-PIMCO Real Return Fund A	1.04%/0.85%	0.87%	1.65%	1.24%	2.94%	
Intermediate-Term Bond						
2287-Metropolitan West Total Rtrn Bd Fd I	0.44%/0.44%	-0.09%	-0.21%	2.49%	5.54%	
Asset Allocation						
Lifecycle						
2179-TRowePrc Retirement 2010 Fund Adv	0.82%/0.82%	0.17%	4.69%	5.93%	5.66%	
2180-TRowePrc Retirement 2015 Fund Adv	0.84%/0.84%	0.34%	5.63%	6.84%	6.22%	
2181-TRowePrc Retirement 2020 Fund Adv	0.88%/0.88%	0.40%	6.80%	7.79%	6.71%	
2182-TRowePrc Retirement 2025 Fund Adv	0.92%/0.92%	0.51%	7.78%	8.61%	7.11%	
2186-TRowePrc Retirement 2030 Fund Adv	0.94%/0.94%	0.66%	8.74%	9.34%	7.49%	
2184-TRowePrc Retirement 2035 Fund Adv	0.97%/0.97%	0.74%	9.41%	9.86%	7.75%	
2185-TRowePrc Retirement 2040 Fund Adv	0.99%/0.99%	0.85%	10.11%	10.25%	7.99%	
2183-TRowePrc Retirement 2045 Fund Adv	0.99%/0.99%	0.87%	10.39%	10.36%	8.04%	
2187-TRowePrc Retirement 2050 Fund Adv	0.99%/0.99%	0.84%	10.39%	10.37%	8.04%	
2188-TRowePrc Retirement 2055 Fund Adv	0.99%/0.99%	0.90%	10.34%	10.35%	8.03%	
Balanced						
Allocation--30% to 50% Equity						
2178-TRowePrc Retirement Balanced Fnd Adv	0.81%/0.81%	0.35%	4.58%	5.08%	5.12%	
Large Cap Value						
Large Blend						
899 -Vanguard 500 Index Fund Adm	0.04%/0.04%	3.42%	14.34%	13.38%	10.16%	
Large Value						

This is an actual retirement statement with the different funds listed. Compare the expense ratios and percentage returns of the Vanguard Index to the other comparable funds.

Average Annual Total Returns as of: 06/30/2018					See Performance Introduction Page for Additiona
Fund Number Investment Options	Gross / Net Fund Expense Ratio *	3-Mo	1-Yr	5-Yr	10-Yr Inception
2876-MFS Value Fund R3	0.84%/0.84%	-0.68%	3.76%	10.39%	8.38%
Large Cap Growth					
Large Growth					
1100-MainStay Large Cap Growth Fund R2	1.10%/1.10%	7.31%	27.14%	15.95%	10.59%
1120-Neuberger Berman Sustain Equity Trst	1.02%/1.02%	3.60%	12.57%	11.79%	8.99%
Small/Mid/Specialty					
Mid-Cap Blend					
2192-JPMorgan Mid Cap Value Fund A	1.26%/1.24%	1.45%	6.20%	10.32%	10.07%
1197-Vanguard Mid-Cap Index Fund Inst	0.04%/0.04%	2.57%	12.10%	12.31%	10.11%
Mid-Cap Growth					
2497-Carillon Eagle Mid Cap Growth Fd A	1.07%/1.07%	3.26%	20.82%	14.93%	10.53%
Small Blend					
1247-Goldman Sachs Sm Cp Value Fnd A	1.36%/1.34%	3.65%	11.65%	11.16%	11.08%
1198-Vanguard Small-Cap Index Fund Inst	0.04%/0.04%	6.21%	16.51%	12.41%	11.29%
Small Growth					
2197-Invesco Small Cap Disc Fnd A	1.40%/1.40%	7.91%	20.64%	12.10%	8.90%
Specialty - Real Estate					
2198-Invesco Real Estate Fund A	1.24%/1.24%	6.87%	4.69%	7.95%	7.25%
Global / International					
Foreign Large Blend					
9859-Vanguard Total Intl Stk Index Fd Adm	0.11%/0.11%	-3.17%	7.10%	6.42%	2.72%
Foreign Large Growth					
498-American Funds EuroPacific R3	1.14%/1.14%	-2.96%	8.67%	7.65%	4.18%

Does a higher cost fund provide better returns?

Make sure to check expense ratios as higher fees can be costly over time. These small numbers matter. Sometimes a difference as small as 0.5%-1.0% can chip away as much as one third of a retirement account.

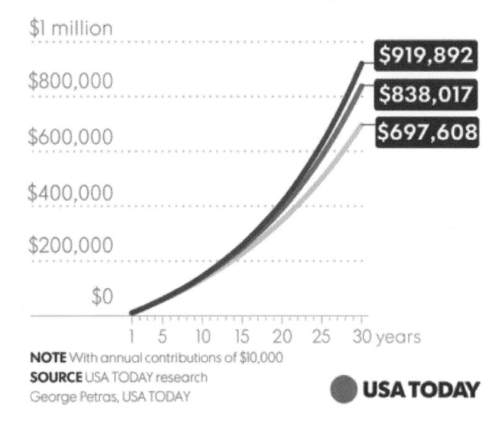

FEES AFFECT SAVINGS OVER TIME

Investing $10,000 a year in a retirement plan that averages 7% returns over 30 years is great. But investing with a 2% fee instead of a 0.5% fee can cost your plan $222,284.

Savings after fees of: ● 0.5% ● 1.0% ● 2.0%

$919,892
$838,017
$697,608

$1 million
$800,000
$600,000
$400,000
$200,000
$0

1 5 10 15 20 25 30 years

NOTE With annual contributions of $10,000
SOURCE USA TODAY research
George Petras, USA TODAY

● USA TODAY

CHAPTER 5: A STEP-BY-STEP GUIDE TO BUYING STOCKS

Sometimes the language of investing can cause people to be discouraged about investing. No worries! I am here to simplify this process as much as possible to reduce the barriers that may prevent people from participating in the stock market. This step by step blueprint takes you through exactly what buttons to press as you invest with your online brokerage account or with an App. I have also clarified some of the terminology as you go through each step so you know exactly what certain terms mean. This visual aid was designed to walk you through the process step-by-step and screen-by-screen.

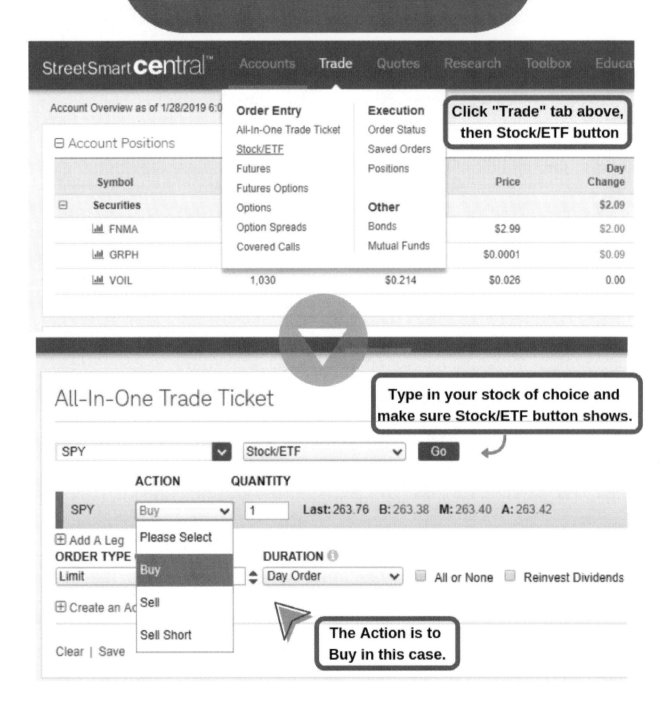

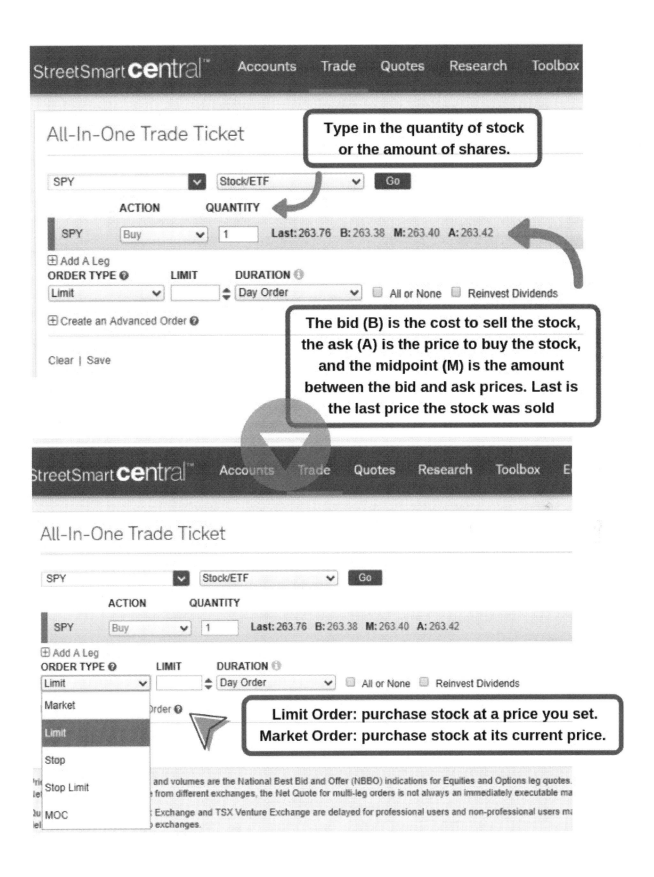

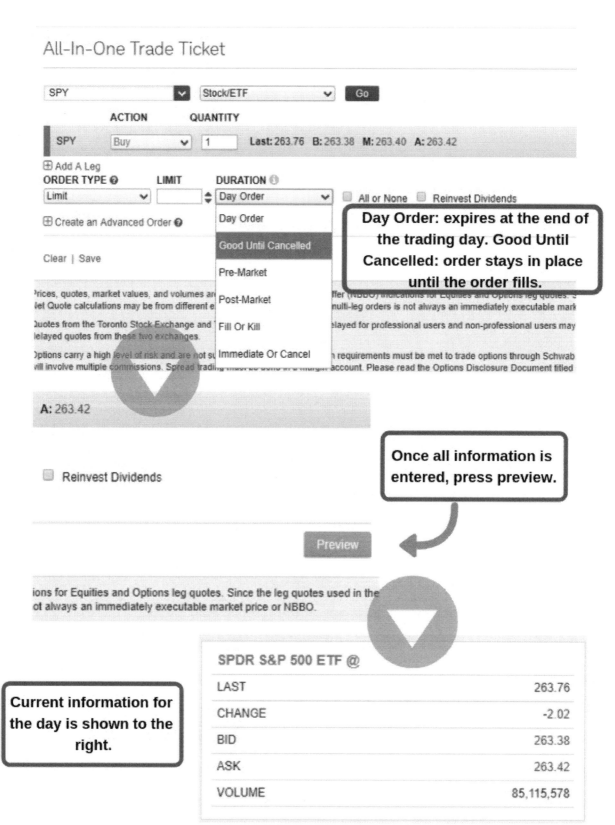

All-In-One Trade Ticket

SPY | Stock/ETF | Go

| | **ACTION** | **QUANTITY** | |
| SPY | Buy | 1 | Last: 263.76 B: 263.38 M: 263.40 A: 263.42 |

⊞ Add A Leg

ORDER TYPE ❷ **LIMIT** **DURATION** ⓘ

Limit | | Day Order | ☐ All or None ☐ Reinvest Dividends

⊞ Create an Advanced Order ❷

Day Order

Good Until Cancelled

Clear | Save

Pre-Market

Post-Market

Fill Or Kill

Immediate Or Cancel

> **Day Order: expires at the end of the trading day. Good Until Cancelled: order stays in place until the order fills.**

Prices, quotes, market values, and volumes are ... fer (NBBO) indications for Equities and Options leg quotes. ...
Net Quote calculations may be from different e... multi-leg orders is not always an immediately executable mark...

Quotes from the Toronto Stock Exchange and ... elayed for professional users and non-professional users may ...
delayed quotes from these two exchanges.

Options carry a high level of risk and are not su... requirements must be met to trade options through Schwab ...
will involve multiple commissions. Spread trading ... account. Please read the Options Disclosure Document titled

A: 263.42

☐ Reinvest Dividends

> **Once all information is entered, press preview.**

Preview

ions for Equities and Options leg quotes. Since the leg quotes used in the ...
ot always an immediately executable market price or NBBO.

> **Current information for the day is shown to the right.**

SPDR S&P 500 ETF @	
LAST	263.76
CHANGE	-2.02
BID	263.38
ASK	263.42
VOLUME	85,115,578

ⓘ The market is now closed. This order will be placed for

This order will be entered for the next standard market
Please be aware that because of extended hours tradin

You are purchasing an Exchange Traded Fund which tr
an exchange. Please read the prospectus carefully befc

All fees and costs of trade will be shown. Click "Place Order" to execute the trade or "Cancel" to make adjustments.

Buy 1 SPY Share @ Limit 263.42, Day Order

Commission:	$4.95
Estimated Order:	$263.42
Estimated Total:	**$268.37**

All-In-One Trade Ticket

Cancel   Place Order

Your order has been submitted.

Order #: 48735354

Please ensure that you check your order status

Please record this order number for your recor

Your order number will be shown for tracking.

Order Time
1/28/2019 6:18:33 PM ET

Place Another Trade

View Order Status | View Positions

You may modify or cancel your order before it is filled.

Balances	Positions	Order Status	Saved

Symbol	Qty	Status
Order Type/Price	Action	☐ Hide cancelled
SPY	1	☐ Open
Limit 263.42	BUY	Modify | Cancel
FNMA	200	☐ Open
Limit 3.20	SELL	Modify | Cancel
CFRX	1000	■ Filled
Limit 0.52	SELL	1000 @ 0.52 Price Improvement $0.63 ❓
CFRX	1000	■ Cancelled
Limit 0.71	SELL	
FNMA	200	■ Filled
Limit 2.92	BUY	200 @ 2.92

Detach ↗

How to buy stocks (from the Robinhood App)

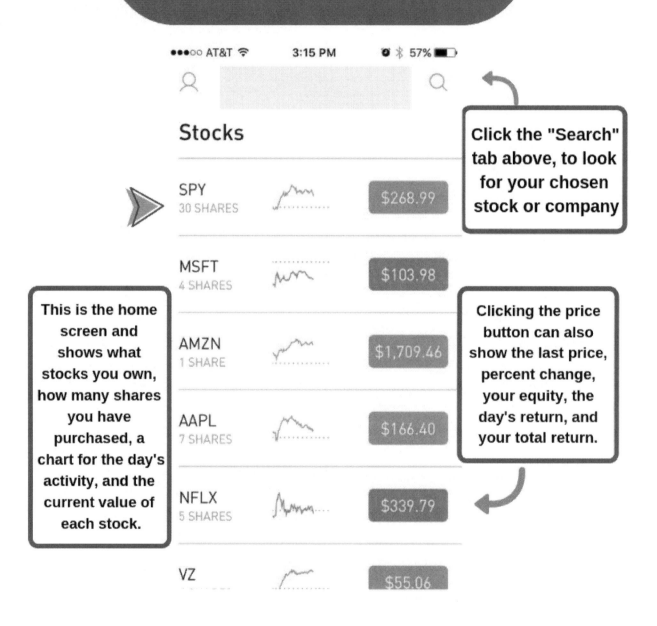

●●●○○ AT&T 📶   3:15 PM   🔘 ⚡ 57% 🔋

Stocks

SPY 30 SHARES		$268.99
MSFT 4 SHARES		$103.98
AMZN 1 SHARE		$1,709.46
AAPL 7 SHARES		$166.40
NFLX 5 SHARES		$339.79
VZ		$55.06

Click the "Search" tab above, to look for your chosen stock or company

This is the home screen and shows what stocks you own, how many shares you have purchased, a chart for the day's activity, and the current value of each stock.

Clicking the price button can also show the last price, percent change, your equity, the day's return, and your total return.

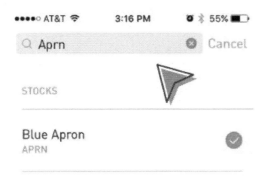

Type the stock symbol in the search box, then select it from the list below

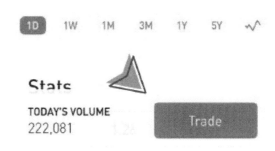

Once clicked, the current price, daily change, and chart will appear. you can scroll for additional information. Select the "Trade" button to purchase.

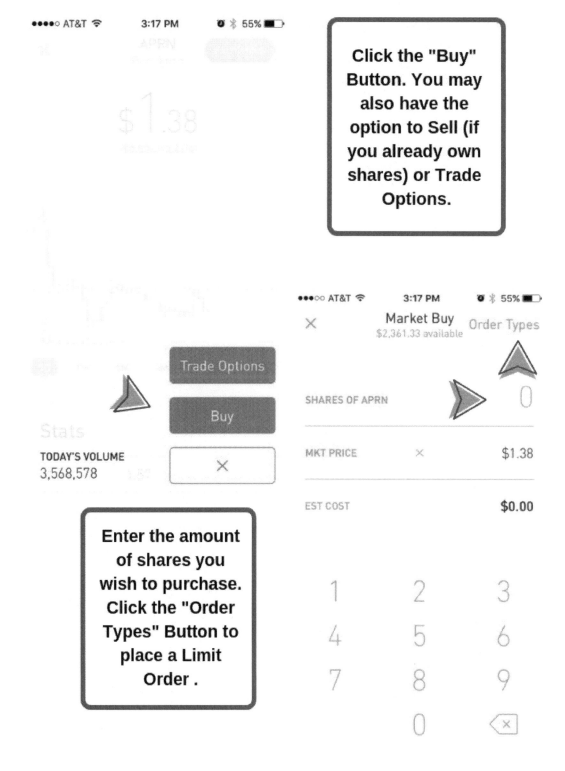

●●●●○ AT&T 🛜   3:17 PM   ⏰ ✳ 55% 🔋

Click the "Buy" Button. You may also have the option to Sell (if you already own shares) or Trade Options.

Trade Options

Buy

✕

Stats

TODAY'S VOLUME
3,568,578

●●●○○ AT&T 🛜   3:17 PM   ⏰ ✳ 55% 🔋

✕   **Market Buy**
$2,361.33 available   Order Types

⌃

SHARES OF APRN   ▶   0

MKT PRICE   ✕ $1.38

EST COST $0.00

Enter the amount of shares you wish to purchase. Click the "Order Types" Button to place a Limit Order .

1	2	3
4	5	6
7	8	9
	0	⌫

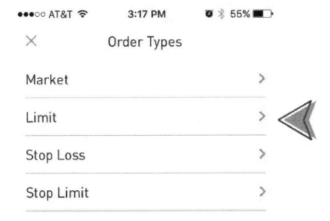

●●●○○ AT&T 📶   3:17 PM   🕐 ✳ 55% 🔋▸

✕   Order Types

Market   ›

Limit   ›

Stop Loss   ›

Stop Limit   ›

Enter the order type you would like. (Typically a Limit order, but Market orders are OK with high volume stocks)

●●●○○ AT&T 📶   3:17 PM   🕐 ✳ 55% 🔋▸

‹ Order Types

Limit Price

Specify the maximum amount
you're willing to pay per share of
APRN.

When placing a Limit order, type in the price you would like to purchase the stock. (The current price is listed for reference)

|$0.00

CURRENT PRICE: $1.38

1   2   3

4   5   6

7   8   9

.   0   ⌫

●●●○○ AT&T 📶   3:17 PM   ⦿ ✳ 55% 🔋

❮ Order Types

Limit Price

Specify the maximum amount
you're willing to pay per share of
APRN.

$1.38

CURRENT PRICE: $1.38

Continue

1	2	3
4	5	6
7	8	9
.	0	⌫

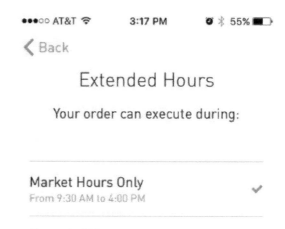

**Type in your price,
then click
"Continue."**

●●●○○ AT&T 📶   3:17 PM   ⦿ ✳ 55% 🔋

❮ Back

Extended Hours

Your order can execute during:

Market Hours Only   ✓
From 9:30 AM to 4:00 PM

Extended Hours
From 9:00 AM to 6:00 PM

**Type in your preference
of hours. Extended
hours include
movement in the stock
outside of the regular
market hours. Click
"Continue."**

Trading during extended hours involves additional
risks like increased price volatility and lower
trading volume.

Continue

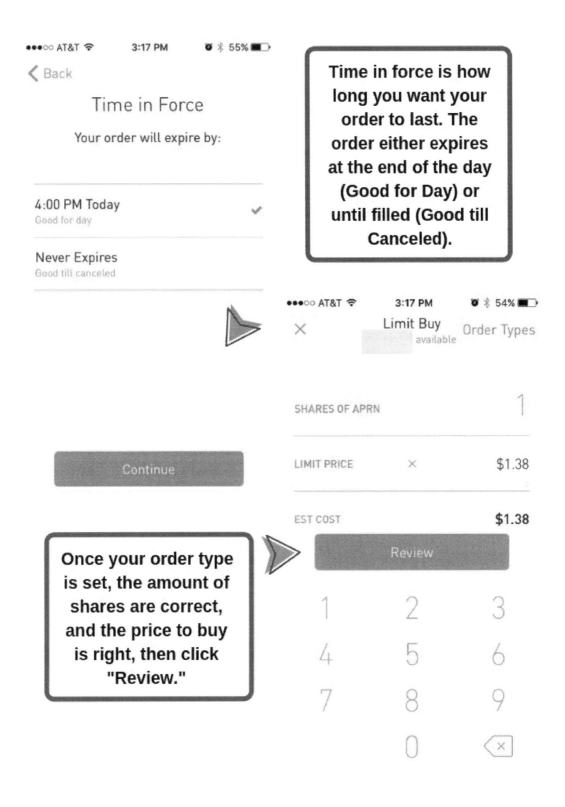

Time in force is how long you want your order to last. The order either expires at the end of the day (Good for Day) or until filled (Good till Canceled).

Once your order type is set, the amount of shares are correct, and the price to buy is right, then click "Review."

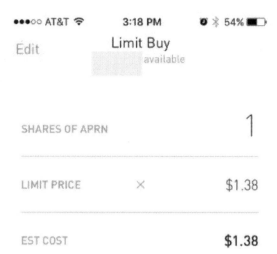

●●●○○ AT&T 🛜   3:18 PM   🔴 ⁑ 54% 🔋

Edit   Limit Buy
                    available

SHARES OF APRN   1

LIMIT PRICE   ✕ $1.38

EST COST $1.38

Click "Edit" if you need to make any changes. If not, swipe up to place your order.

Order Summary

You are placing a good for day limit order to buy 1 share of APRN. Your pending order, if executed, will execute at $1.38 per share or better.

Swipe up to submit

The confirmation screen confirms your order. Notice commissions are $0 which is why this App is useful (they can be $5+ per trade).

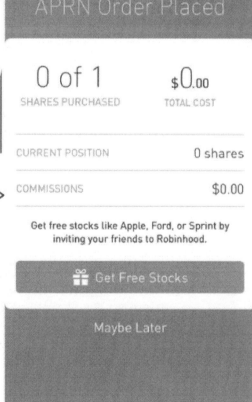

●●●○○ AT&T 🛜   3:18 PM   🔴 ⁑ 54% 🔋

APRN Order Placed

0 of 1 $0.00
SHARES PURCHASED   TOTAL COST

CURRENT POSITION   0 shares

COMMISSIONS $0.00

Get free stocks like Apple, Ford, or Sprint by inviting your friends to Robinhood.

🎁 Get Free Stocks

Maybe Later

Once your stock is purchased you can see what you bought it for (avg. cost) and how much it is worth.

Your Position

SHARES	EQUITY
1	$1.39
AVG COST	PORTFOLIO DIVERSITY
$1.38	0.00%

TODAY'S VOLUME
3,569,078

Trade

You can see that my stock had appreciated by one cent since I bought it. Price can fluctuate every second.You can scroll down to see all available stock information.

●●●●○ AT&T 📶   3:19 PM   🔋 ⚡ 54% ■

✕   APRN — $1.39   WATCHING
Blue Apron

Your Position

SHARES	EQUITY
1	$1.39
AVG COST	PORTFOLIO DIVERSITY
$1.38	0.00%
TODAY'S RETURN	+$0.0100 (+0.72%)
TOTAL RETURN	+$0.0100 (+0.72%)

Stats

OPEN	1.57	VOLUME	3.57M
HIGH	1.59	AVG VOL	2.78M

TODAY'S VOLUME
3,569,078

Trade

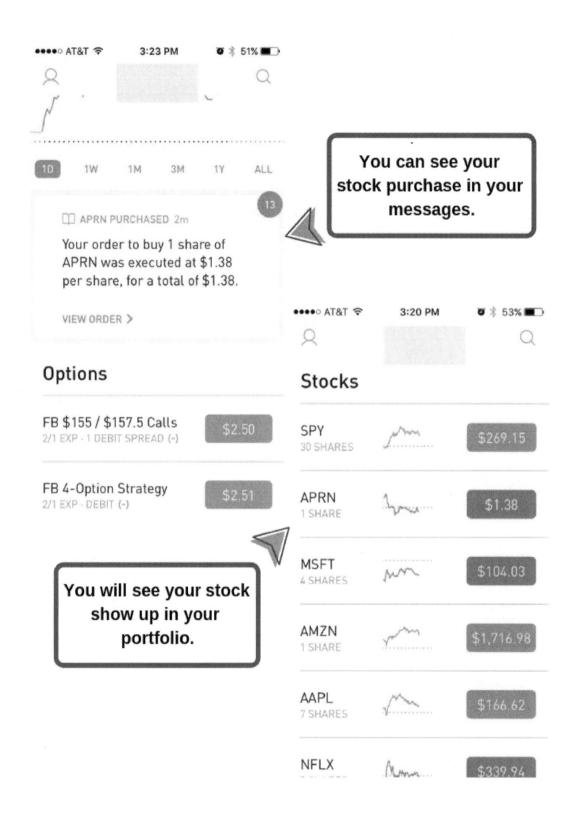

How to sell stocks (from the Robinhood App)

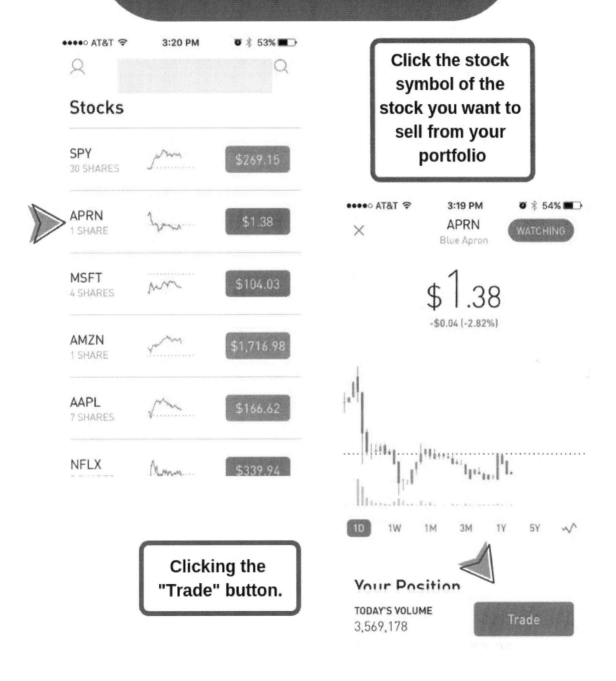

Click the stock symbol of the stock you want to sell from your portfolio

Clicking the "Trade" button.

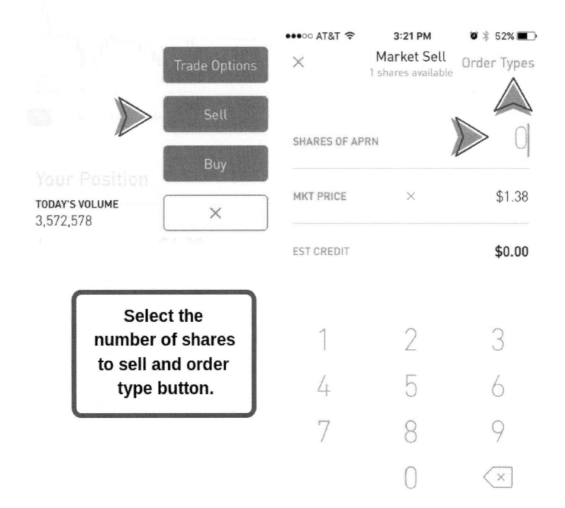

●●●○○ AT&T 🛜   3:22 PM   🔘 ⚡ 52% 🔋

✕   Order Types

Market   >

Limit   >

Stop Loss   >

Stop Limit   >

Select the order type.

Select the price you want to sell your stock if you are using a limit order.

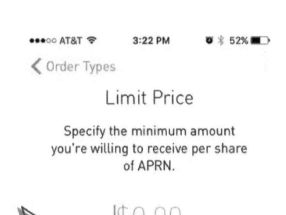

●●●○○ AT&T 🛜   3:22 PM   🔘 ⚡ 52% 🔋

❮ Order Types

Limit Price

Specify the minimum amount
you're willing to receive per share
of APRN.

|$0.00

CURRENT PRICE: $1.39

1	2	3
4	5	6
7	8	9
.	0	⊗

●●●○○ AT&T 📶   3:22 PM   📷 ∗ 52% 🔋

‹ Order Types

Limit Price

Specify the minimum amount
you're willing to receive per share
of APRN.

$1.39

CURRENT PRICE: $1.39

Continue

1	2	3
4	5	6
7	8	9
.	0	⌫

**Once your price
is selected, click
"Continue."**

●●●○○ AT&T 📶   3:22 PM   📷 ∗ 51% 🔋

✕   **Limit Sell**   Order Types
      1 shares available

SHARES OF APRN   1

LIMIT PRICE   ✕ $1.39

EST CREDIT $1.39

Review

**Once your price
is selected, click
"Review."**

1	2	3
4	5	6
7	8	9
	0	⌫

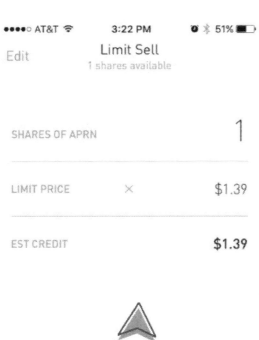

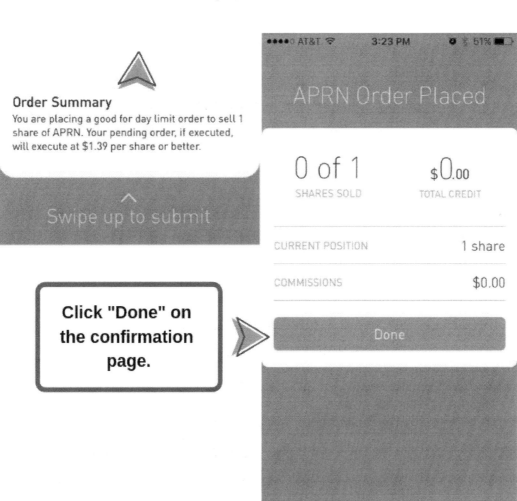

Swipe Up to execute your sell order.

Order Summary
You are placing a good for day limit order to sell 1 share of APRN. Your pending order, if executed, will execute at $1.39 per share or better.

Swipe up to submit

Click "Done" on the confirmation page.

You can click on the Pending Orders to see the details of your trade/transaction.

Pending Orders

| Limit Sell | Placed |
| Jan 31, 2019 | 1 share |

Stats

| OPEN | 1.57 | VOLUME | 3.58M |

TODAY'S VOLUME
3,579,202

Trade

You have the option to cancel the order if it has not yet been filled.

●●●●○ AT&T 🤝   3:23 PM   🔘 ⚡ 51% 🔋

⟨ Back   Order Details

Blue Apron

TYPE	Limit Sell
TIME IN FORCE	Good for day
SUBMITTED	Jan 31, 2019
STATUS	Placed
LIMIT PRICE	$1.39
ENTERED QUANTITY	1

 Cancel Order

●●●●○ AT&T 🔆   3:23 PM   ⏰ ✳ 51% ▮▮▮◻

‹ Back   Order Details

Blue Apron

TYPE	Limit Sell
TIME IN FORCE	Good for day
SUBMITTED	Jan 31, 2019
STATUS	Filled
LIMIT PRICE	$1.39
ENTERED QUANTITY	1
FILLED	Jan 31, 2019 at 3:22 PM ET
FILLED QUANTITY	1 share at $1.39
TOTAL NOTIONAL	$1.39

Once the order is filled/ executed, it will show up in your history and on your messages.

●●●●○ AT&T 🔆   4:43 PM   ⏰ ✳ 22% ◻▮+

👤   🔍

| 1D | 1W | 1M | 3M | 1Y | ALL |

📖 APRN SOLD   1h   ⑬

Your order to sell 1 share of APRN was executed at $1.39 per share. Your account was credited $1.39.

VIEW ORDER ›

Options

AMZN $1,780 / $1,785 Calls $0.15
2/1 EXP · 1 DEBIT SPREAD

CHAPTER 6: TAKING THINGS TO THE NEXT LEVEL

Now that you have a start on being able to invest for yourself, there are other things to learn as well. First, you never want to stop learning as change seems to be a constant throughout history. Second, make sure to remain consistent with your strategy. Sometimes, those who go in and out of the market tend to miss some of the best days in the market. If you miss enough of those good days, the average ten percent yearly return that the market benchmark, the S&P 500, gets can easily shrink (it can even lead to negative returns). Third, make sure to add options to your investment knowledge. While you may not want to use them exclusively, they can be used to enhance your stock holdings in a variety of ways. Two strategies that you should learn about are using puts as protection (known as the "protective put" strategy) and using calls to bring in additional income to your stock portfolio (known as the "covered call" strategy). Both of these strategies have various layers to them, so make sure you learn the details of these strategies before you start using them. It could be worth the investment to get this knowledge if you want to take your stock investing to the next level.

At the end of the day, you can get as simple or as complex as you would like with investments and it is all personal preference.

APPENDIX A: GOAL SETTING

Goal setting is a critical component to building wealth. In order to reach your financial destination, you must have a plan to get there. I have included some goal setting documents for your use in setting and accomplishing your personal financial goals. Go through these by yourself or with your significant other to set a standard of accountability.

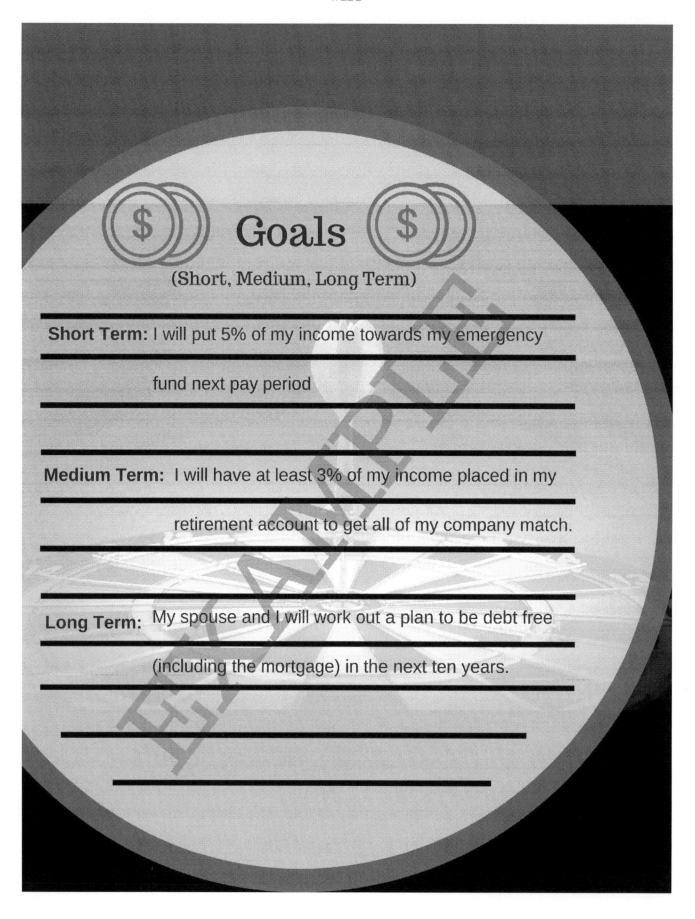

Goals

(Short, Medium, Long Term)

Short Term: I will put 5% of my income towards my emergency fund next pay period

Medium Term: I will have at least 3% of my income placed in my retirement account to get all of my company match.

Long Term: My spouse and I will work out a plan to be debt free (including the mortgage) in the next ten years.

Goals

(Short, Medium, Long Term)

Short Term:

_____

_____

_____

Medium Term:

_____

_____

_____

Long Term:

_____

_____

_____

Goals

(Short, Medium, Long Term)

Short Term:

Medium Term:

Long Term:

Goals

(Short, Medium, Long Term)

Short Term:

Medium Term:

Long Term:

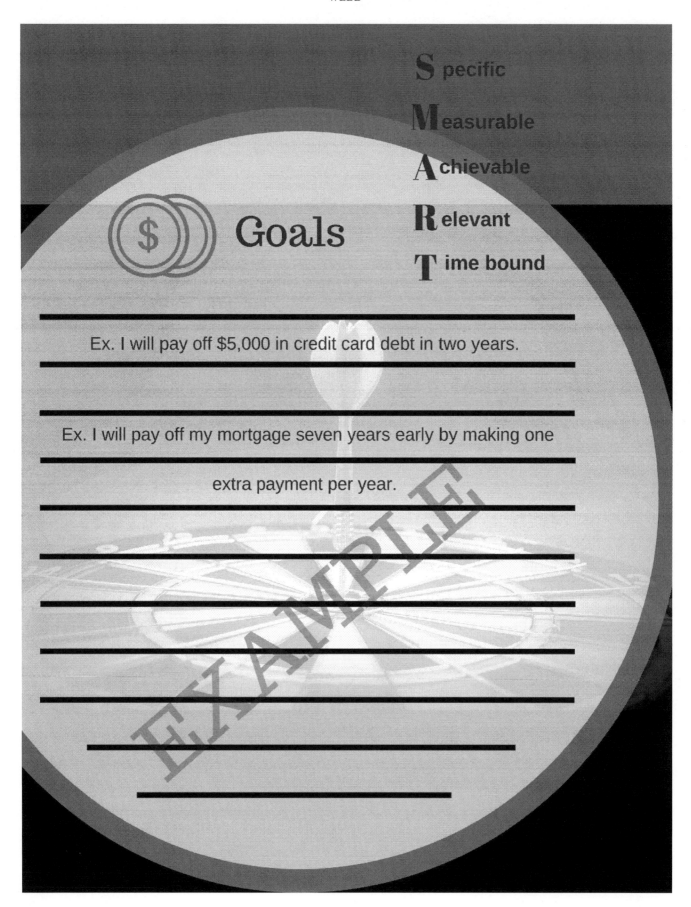

Specific

Measurable

Achievable

Relevant

Time bound

Goals

Ex. I will pay off $5,000 in credit card debt in two years.

Ex. I will pay off my mortgage seven years early by making one

extra payment per year.

S pecific

M easurable

A chievable

R elevant

T ime bound

Goals

S pecific

M easurable

A chievable

R elevant

T ime bound

$ Goals

S pecific

M easurable

A chievable

R elevant

T ime bound

Goals

APPENDIX B: BUDGETING/SPENDING PLANS

Budgets and spending plans are the cornerstone of your financial plan. Having these documents are the first step in gaining control of your finances. Tracking the flow of money coming in and out of your life can be an eye-opening exercise. It allows you to see exactly where each of your hard-earned dollars goes throughout the month and empowers you to take control of your money flow.

I have included some documents to get you started with your budget for a year. These forms are designed to assist you with budgeting and adjusting your spending habits over time.

Budget Spending Plan

Income

List all income →

Monthly Income 1 _____
Monthly Income 2 _____
Other _____
Other _____

Bills

Rent/ Mortgage _____
Car Payment 1 _____
Car Payment 2 _____
Auto Insurance _____
Electric _____
Gas _____
Water/Sewer _____
Student Loans _____
Credit Card 1 _____
Credit Card 2 _____
Credit Card 3 _____
_____ _____

Groceries _____
Cell Phone _____
Entertainment _____
Tithe/Giving _____
Miscellaneous _____
Life Insurance _____
_____ _____
_____ _____
_____ _____
_____ _____
_____ _____

List all expenses ↑

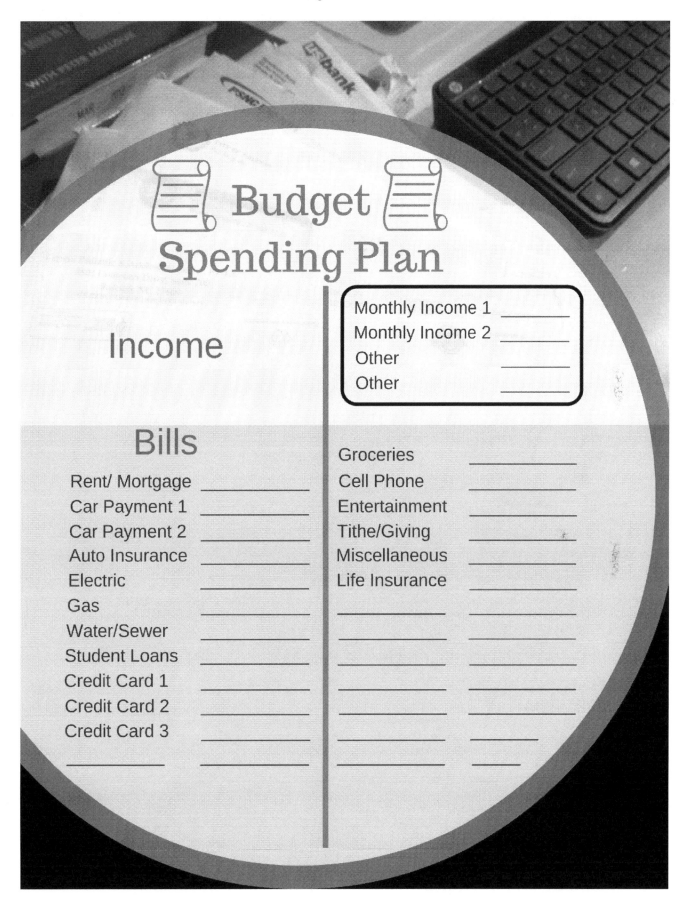

Budget
Spending Plan

Income

Monthly Income 1 _____
Monthly Income 2 _____
Other _____
Other _____

Bills

Rent/ Mortgage _____
Car Payment 1 _____
Car Payment 2 _____
Auto Insurance _____
Electric _____
Gas _____
Water/Sewer _____
Student Loans _____
Credit Card 1 _____
Credit Card 2 _____
Credit Card 3 _____
_____ _____

Groceries _____
Cell Phone _____
Entertainment _____
Tithe/Giving _____
Miscellaneous _____
Life Insurance _____
_____ _____
_____ _____
_____ _____
_____ _____
_____ _____

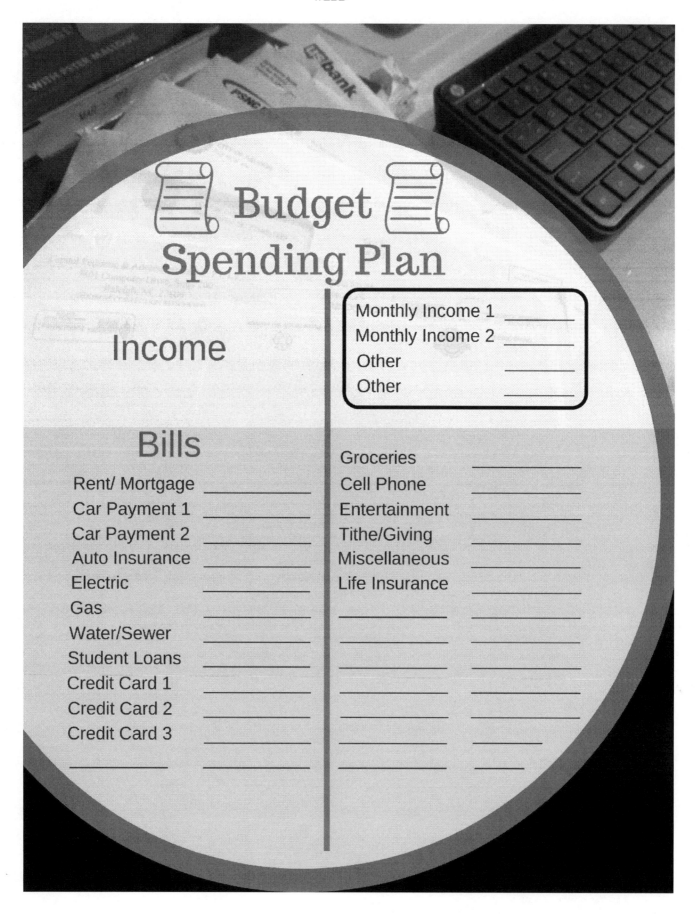

Budget Spending Plan

Income

Monthly Income 1 _____
Monthly Income 2 _____
Other _____
Other _____

Bills

Rent/ Mortgage _____
Car Payment 1 _____
Car Payment 2 _____
Auto Insurance _____
Electric _____
Gas _____
Water/Sewer _____
Student Loans _____
Credit Card 1 _____
Credit Card 2 _____
Credit Card 3 _____
_____ _____

Groceries _____
Cell Phone _____
Entertainment _____
Tithe/Giving _____
Miscellaneous _____
Life Insurance _____
_____ _____
_____ _____
_____ _____
_____ _____
_____ _____
_____ _____

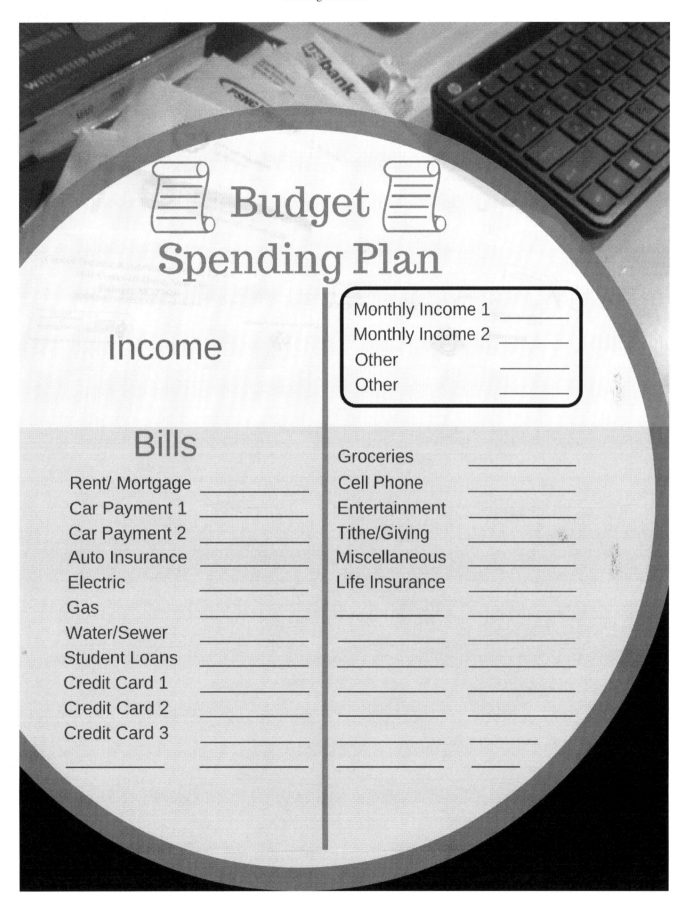

Budget Spending Plan

Income

Monthly Income 1 _____
Monthly Income 2 _____
Other _____
Other _____

Bills

Rent/ Mortgage _____
Car Payment 1 _____
Car Payment 2 _____
Auto Insurance _____
Electric _____
Gas _____
Water/Sewer _____
Student Loans _____
Credit Card 1 _____
Credit Card 2 _____
Credit Card 3 _____
_____ _____

Groceries _____
Cell Phone _____
Entertainment _____
Tithe/Giving _____
Miscellaneous _____
Life Insurance _____
_____ _____
_____ _____
_____ _____
_____ _____

Budget Spending Plan

Income

Monthly Income 1 _____
Monthly Income 2 _____
Other _____
Other _____

Bills

Rent/ Mortgage _____
Car Payment 1 _____
Car Payment 2 _____
Auto Insurance _____
Electric _____
Gas _____
Water/Sewer _____
Student Loans _____
Credit Card 1 _____
Credit Card 2 _____
Credit Card 3 _____
_____ _____

Groceries _____
Cell Phone _____
Entertainment _____
Tithe/Giving _____
Miscellaneous _____
Life Insurance _____
_____ _____
_____ _____
_____ _____
_____ _____
_____ _____
_____ _____

Budget
Spending Plan

Income

Monthly Income 1 _____
Monthly Income 2 _____
Other _____
Other _____

Bills

Rent/ Mortgage _____
Car Payment 1 _____
Car Payment 2 _____
Auto Insurance _____
Electric _____
Gas _____
Water/Sewer _____
Student Loans _____
Credit Card 1 _____
Credit Card 2 _____
Credit Card 3 _____
_____

Groceries _____
Cell Phone _____
Entertainment _____
Tithe/Giving _____
Miscellaneous _____
Life Insurance _____

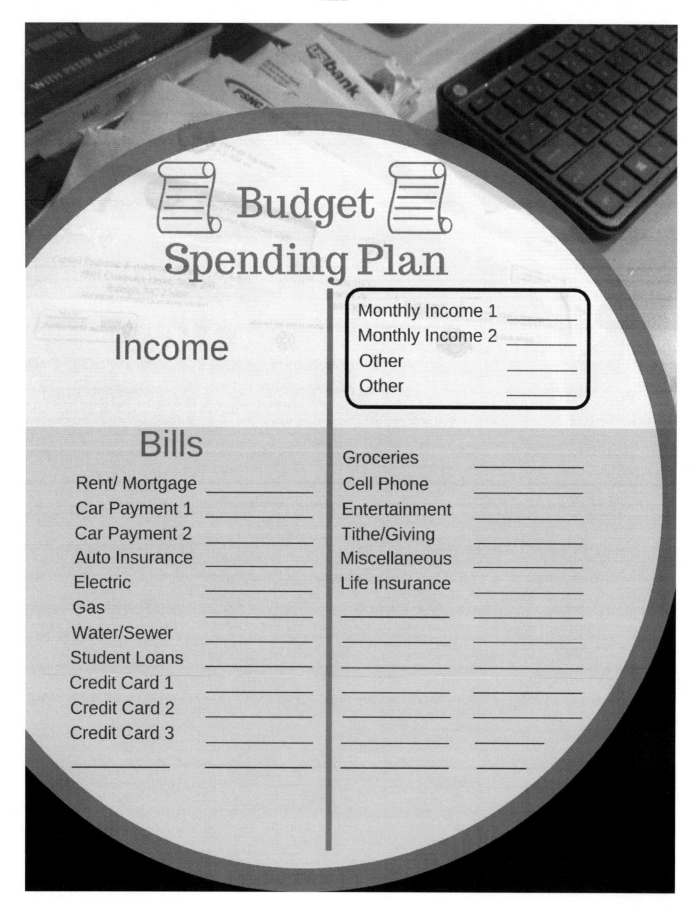

Budget
Spending Plan

Income

Monthly Income 1 _____
Monthly Income 2 _____
Other _____
Other _____

Bills

Rent/ Mortgage _____
Car Payment 1 _____
Car Payment 2 _____
Auto Insurance _____
Electric _____
Gas _____
Water/Sewer _____
Student Loans _____
Credit Card 1 _____
Credit Card 2 _____
Credit Card 3 _____
_____ _____

Groceries _____ _____
Cell Phone _____ _____
Entertainment _____ _____
Tithe/Giving _____ _____
Miscellaneous _____ _____
Life Insurance _____ _____
_____ _____
_____ _____
_____ _____
_____ _____
_____ _____

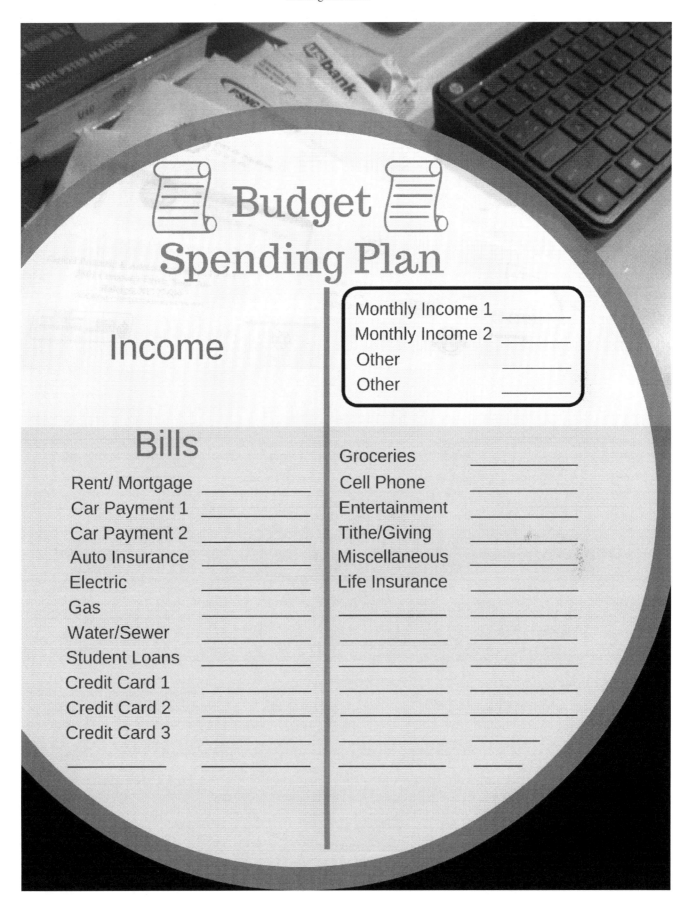

Budget Spending Plan

Income

Monthly Income 1 _____
Monthly Income 2 _____
Other   _____
Other   _____

Bills

Rent/ Mortgage _____
Car Payment 1 _____
Car Payment 2 _____
Auto Insurance _____
Electric _____
Gas _____
Water/Sewer _____
Student Loans _____
Credit Card 1 _____
Credit Card 2 _____
Credit Card 3 _____
_____ _____

Groceries _____
Cell Phone _____
Entertainment _____
Tithe/Giving _____
Miscellaneous _____
Life Insurance _____
_____ _____
_____ _____
_____ _____
_____ _____
_____ _____

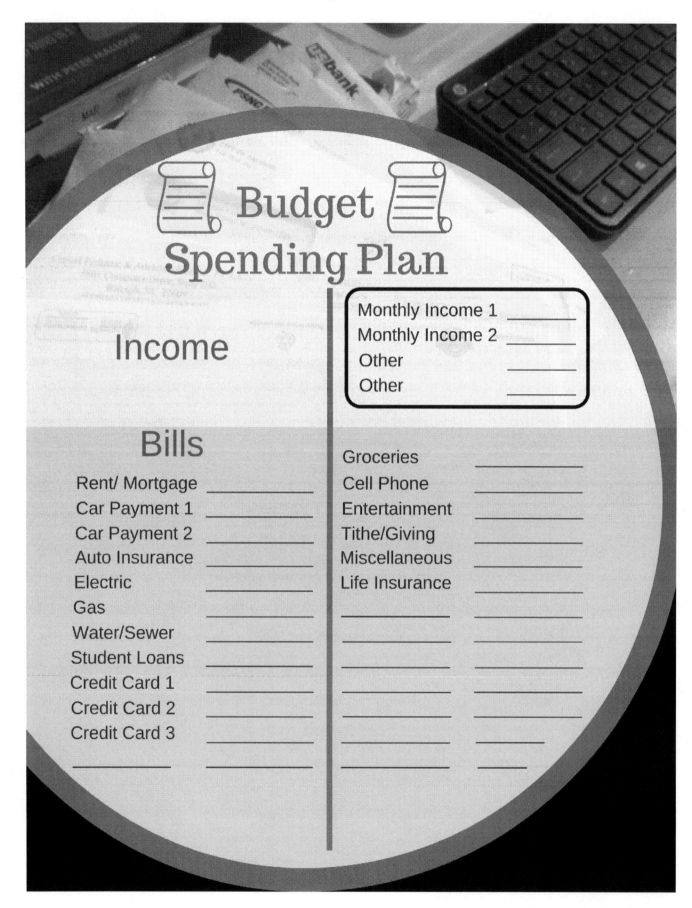

Budget Spending Plan

Income

Monthly Income 1 _____

Monthly Income 2 _____

Other _____

Other _____

Bills

Rent/ Mortgage _____

Car Payment 1 _____

Car Payment 2 _____

Auto Insurance _____

Electric _____

Gas _____

Water/Sewer _____

Student Loans _____

Credit Card 1 _____

Credit Card 2 _____

Credit Card 3 _____

_____ _____

Groceries _____

Cell Phone _____

Entertainment _____

Tithe/Giving _____

Miscellaneous _____

Life Insurance _____

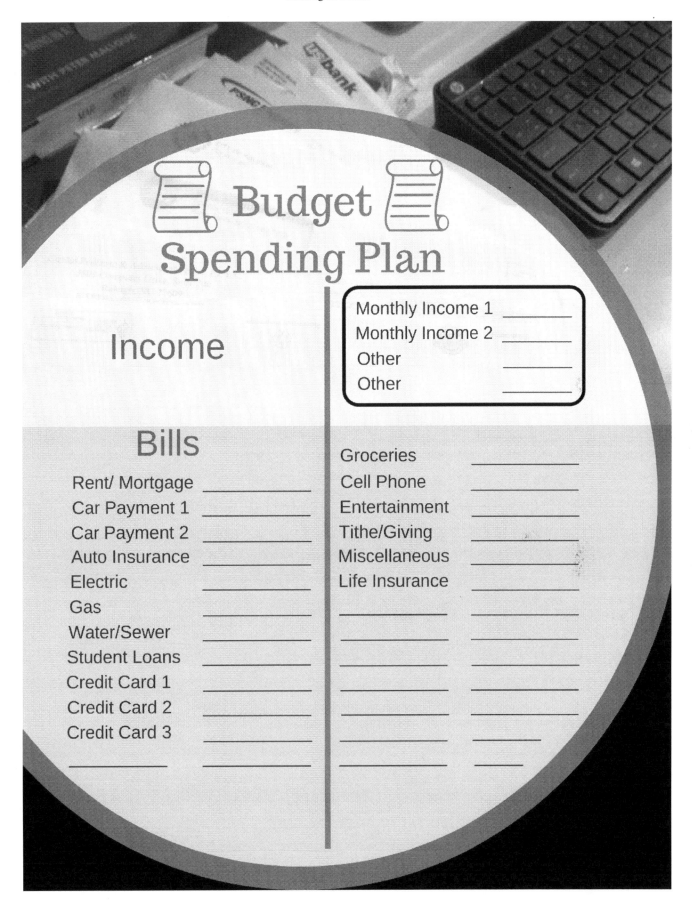

Budget Spending Plan

Income

Monthly Income 1 _____
Monthly Income 2 _____
Other _____
Other _____

Bills

Rent/ Mortgage _____
Car Payment 1 _____
Car Payment 2 _____
Auto Insurance _____
Electric _____
Gas _____
Water/Sewer _____
Student Loans _____
Credit Card 1 _____
Credit Card 2 _____
Credit Card 3 _____
_____ _____

Groceries _____
Cell Phone _____
Entertainment _____
Tithe/Giving _____
Miscellaneous _____
Life Insurance _____
_____ _____
_____ _____
_____ _____
_____ _____
_____ _____
_____ _____

Budget Spending Plan

Income

Monthly Income 1 _____
Monthly Income 2 _____
Other _____
Other _____

Bills

Rent/ Mortgage _____	Groceries _____
Car Payment 1 _____	Cell Phone _____
Car Payment 2 _____	Entertainment _____
Auto Insurance _____	Tithe/Giving _____
Electric _____	Miscellaneous _____
Gas _____	Life Insurance _____
Water/Sewer _____	_____
Student Loans _____	_____
Credit Card 1 _____	_____
Credit Card 2 _____	_____
Credit Card 3 _____	_____
_____	_____

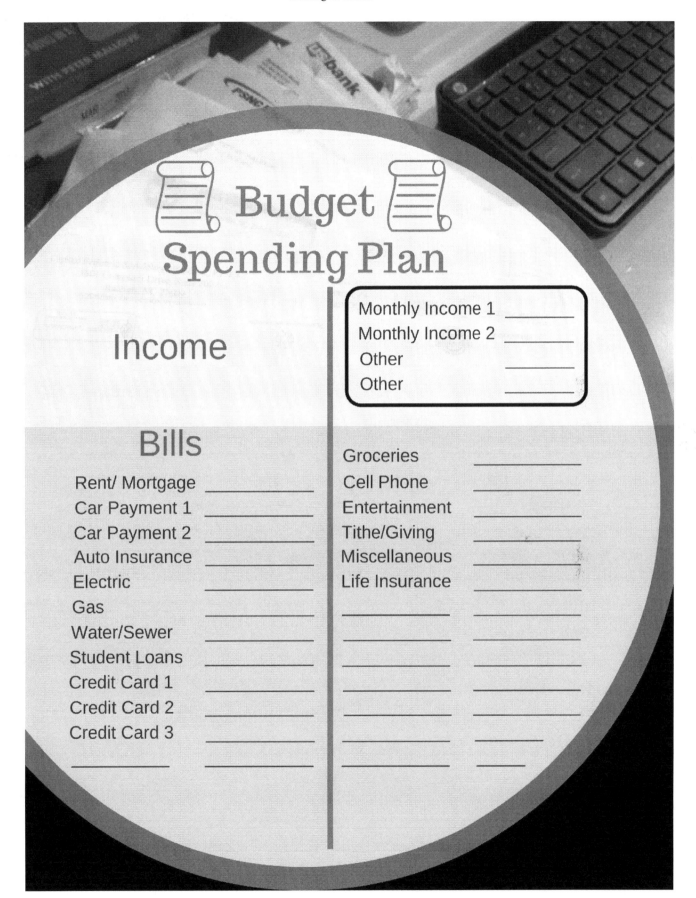

Budget Spending Plan

Income

Monthly Income 1 _____
Monthly Income 2 _____
Other _____
Other _____

Bills

Rent/ Mortgage _____
Car Payment 1 _____
Car Payment 2 _____
Auto Insurance _____
Electric _____
Gas _____
Water/Sewer _____
Student Loans _____
Credit Card 1 _____
Credit Card 2 _____
Credit Card 3 _____
_____ _____

Groceries _____
Cell Phone _____
Entertainment _____
Tithe/Giving _____
Miscellaneous _____
Life Insurance _____

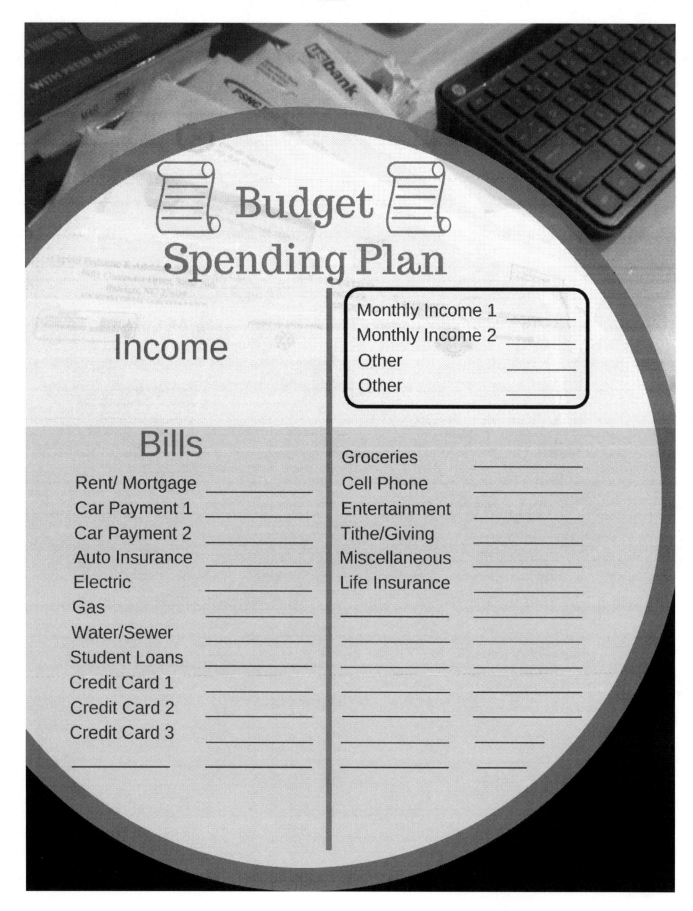

Budget Spending Plan

Income

Monthly Income 1 _____
Monthly Income 2 _____
Other _____
Other _____

Bills

Rent/ Mortgage _____
Car Payment 1 _____
Car Payment 2 _____
Auto Insurance _____
Electric _____
Gas _____
Water/Sewer _____
Student Loans _____
Credit Card 1 _____
Credit Card 2 _____
Credit Card 3 _____
_____ _____

Groceries _____
Cell Phone _____
Entertainment _____
Tithe/Giving _____
Miscellaneous _____
Life Insurance _____
_____ _____
_____ _____
_____ _____
_____ _____
_____ _____

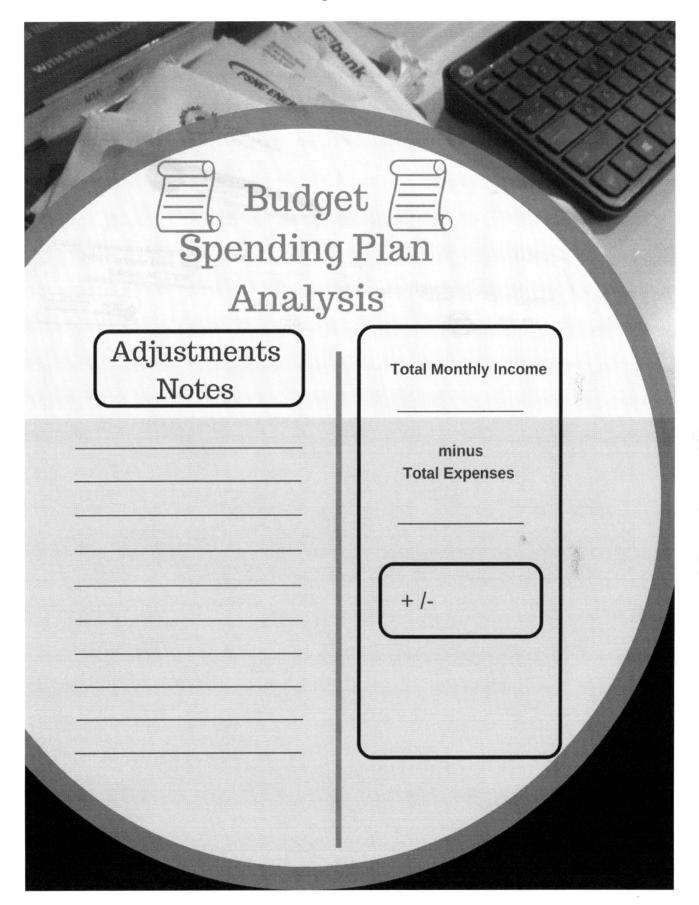

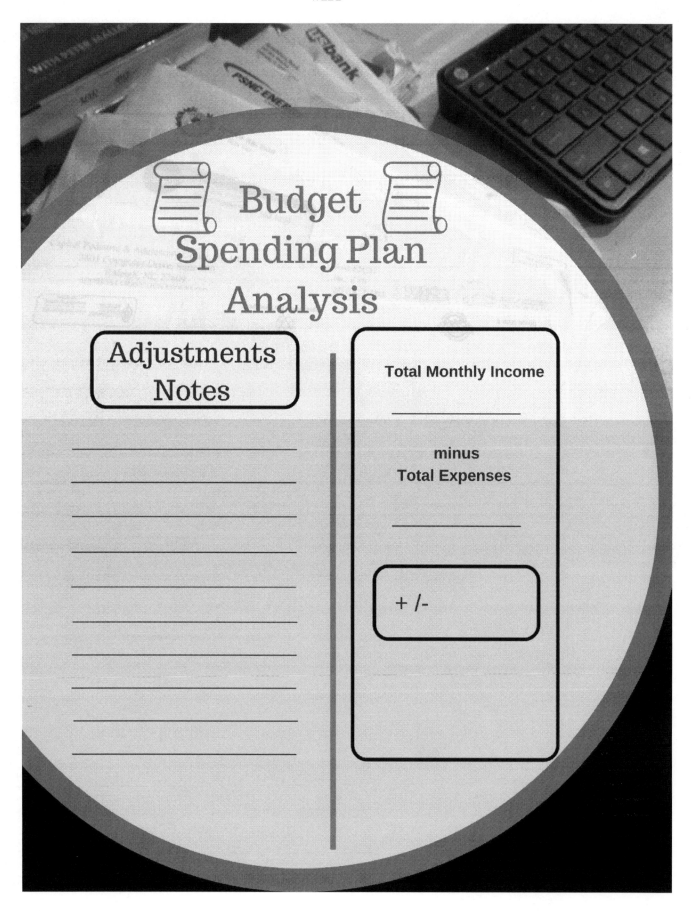

Budget Spending Plan Analysis

Adjustments Notes

Total Monthly Income

_____

minus
Total Expenses

_____

+ /-

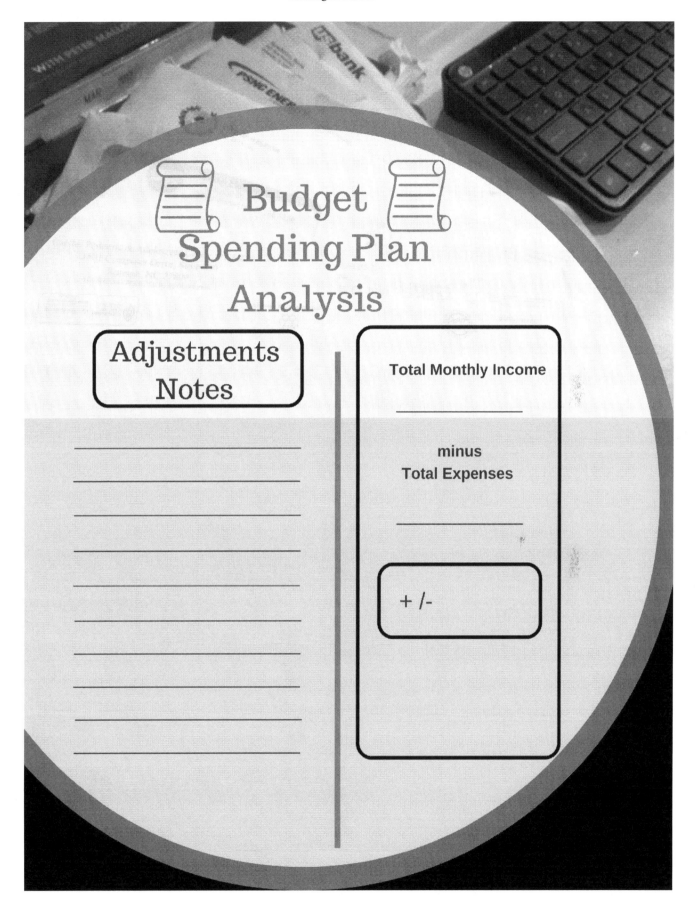

Budget
Spending Plan
Analysis

Adjustments Notes

Total Monthly Income

minus
Total Expenses

+ /-

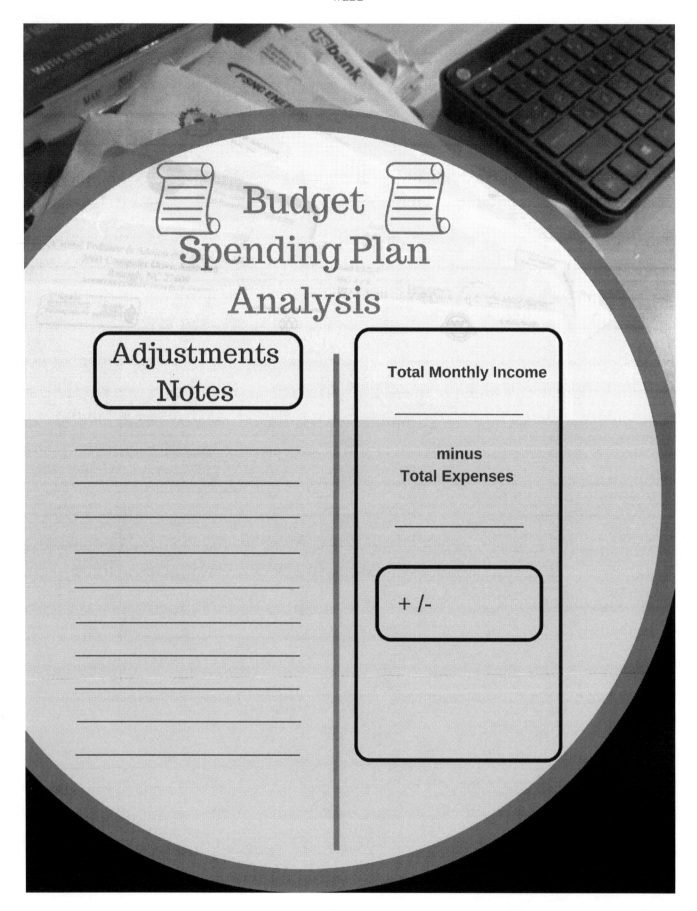

Budget Spending Plan Analysis

Adjustments Notes

Total Monthly Income

_____

minus
Total Expenses

_____

+ /-

APPENDIX C: DEBT REDUCTION

Debt reduction is an integral part of achieving financial freedom. After you complete a budget and are aware of how much additional money you have available to put to use, you need a plan of attack for debt reduction and investing. While both of these can be done simultaneously, you want to make sure to allocate this extra money strategically to accomplish your financial goals.

These debt reduction forms are included to assist you in focusing your extra money on meeting these goals.

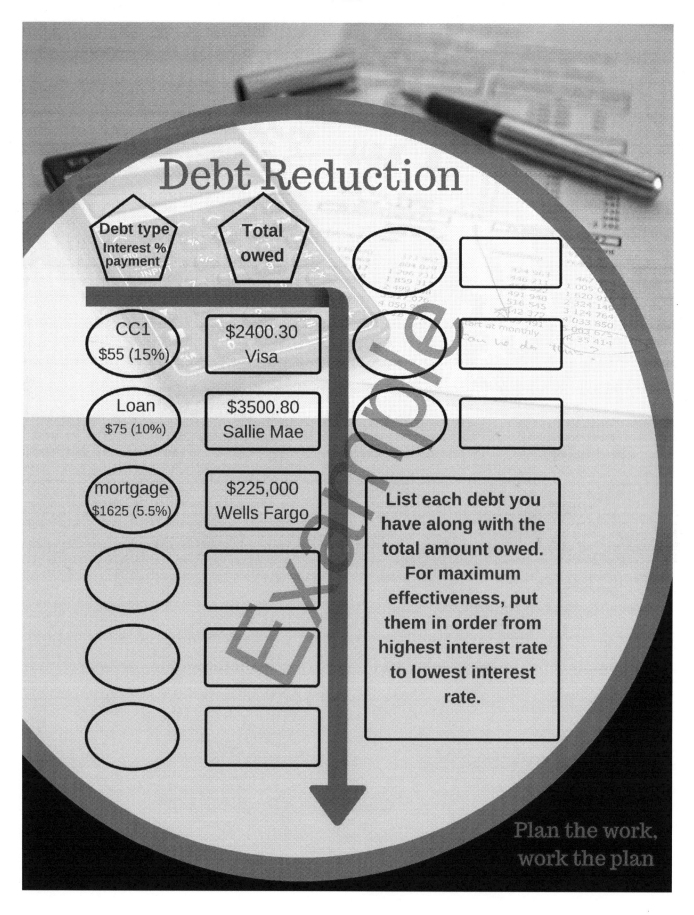

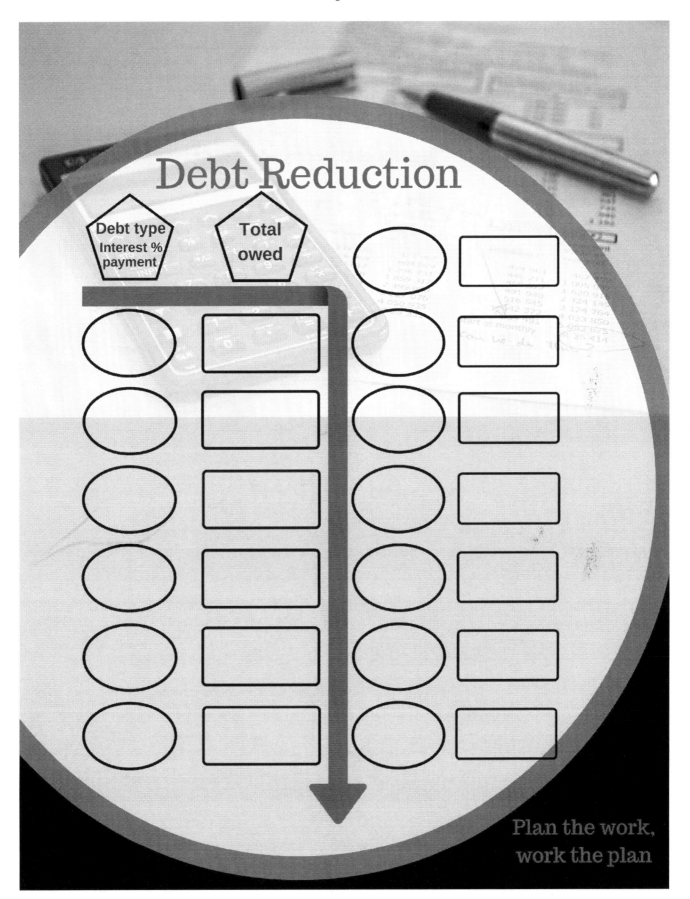

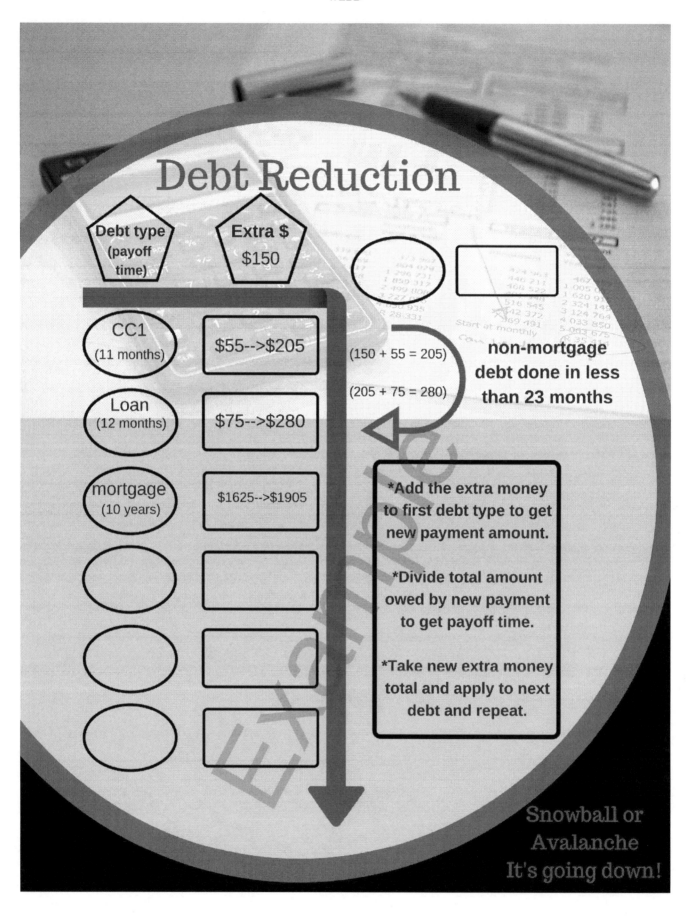

Debt Reduction

Debt type (payoff time)

Extra $ $150

CC1 (11 months) — $55-->$205

Loan (12 months) — $75-->$280

mortgage (10 years) — $1625-->$1905

(150 + 55 = 205)

(205 + 75 = 280)

non-mortgage debt done in less than 23 months

*Add the extra money to first debt type to get new payment amount.

*Divide total amount owed by new payment to get payoff time.

*Take new extra money total and apply to next debt and repeat.

Snowball or Avalanche It's going down!

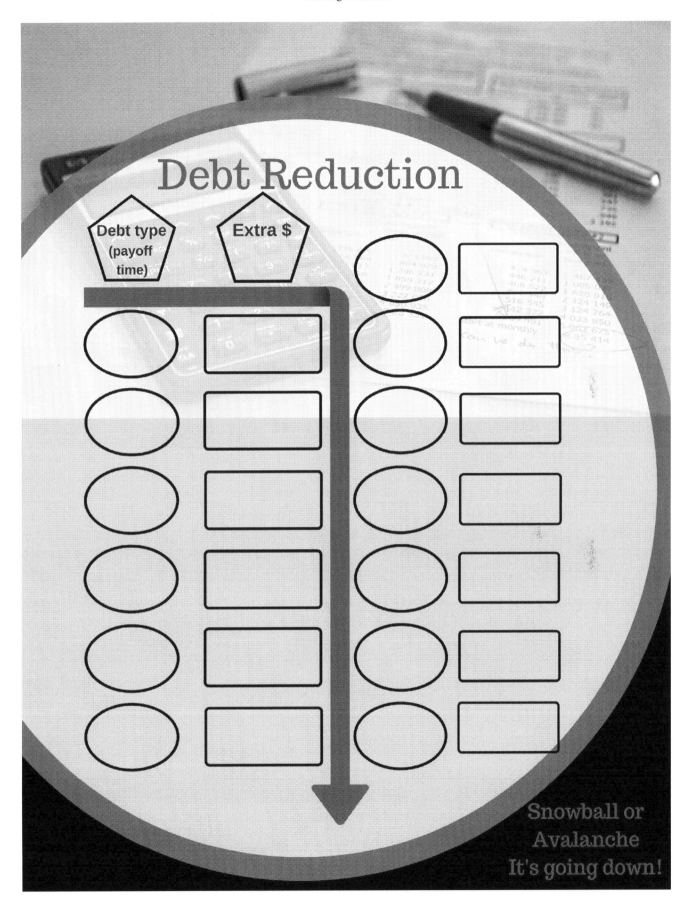

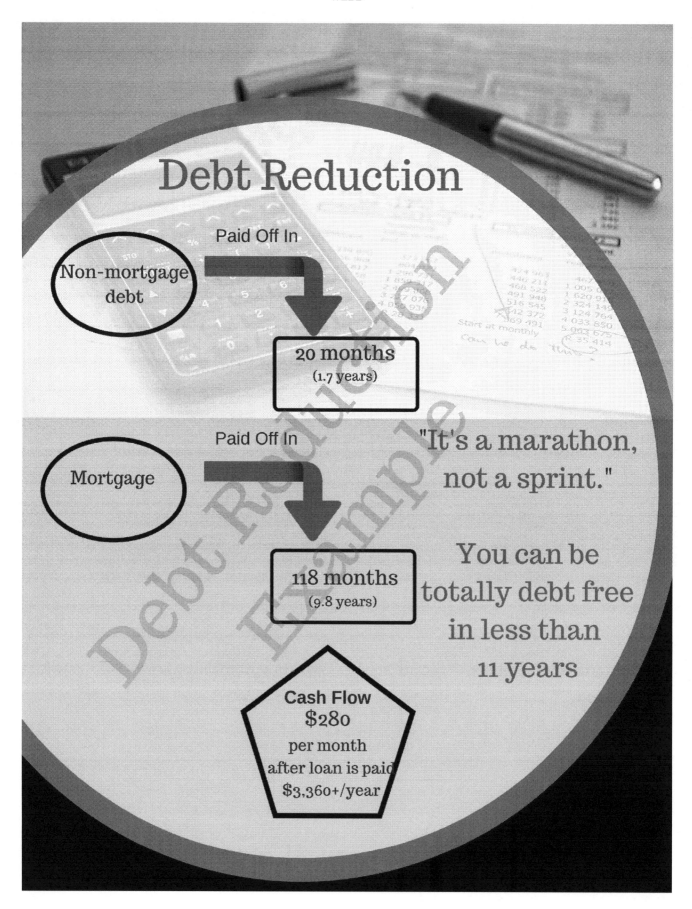

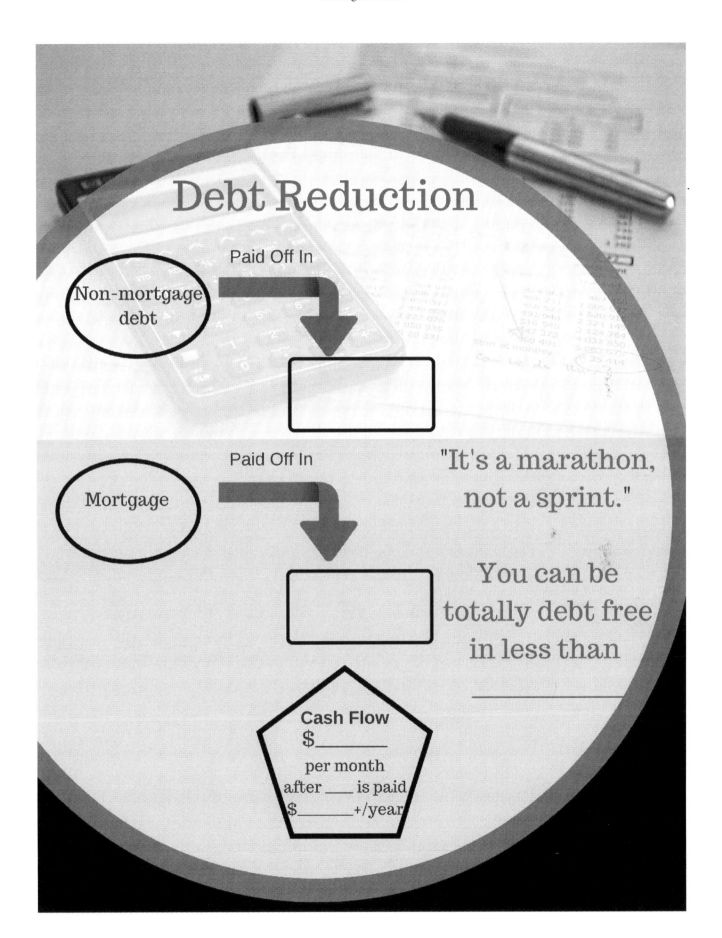

APPENDIX D: NOTES

Notes

All money is now hard at work for you!

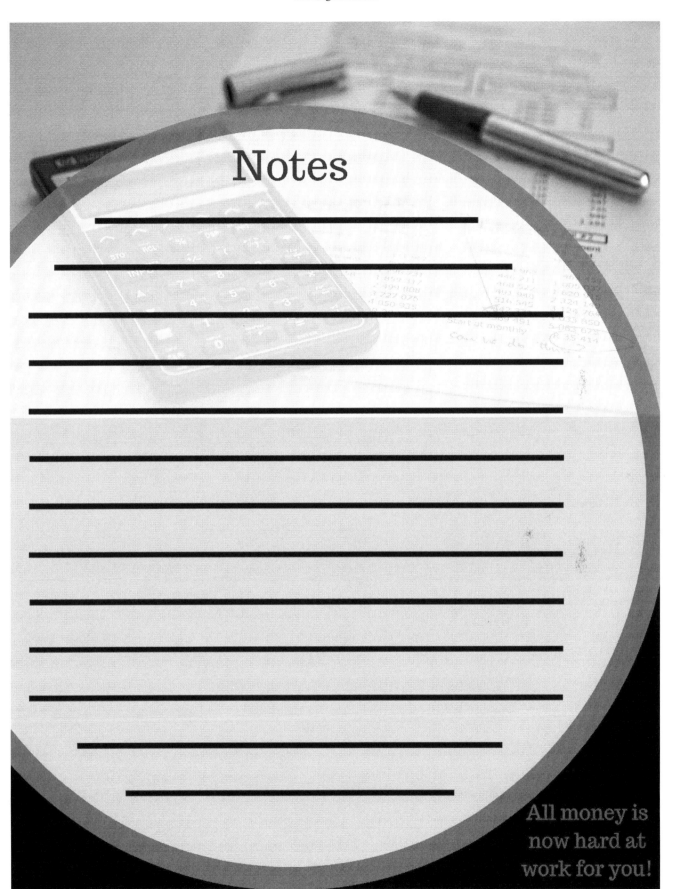

Notes

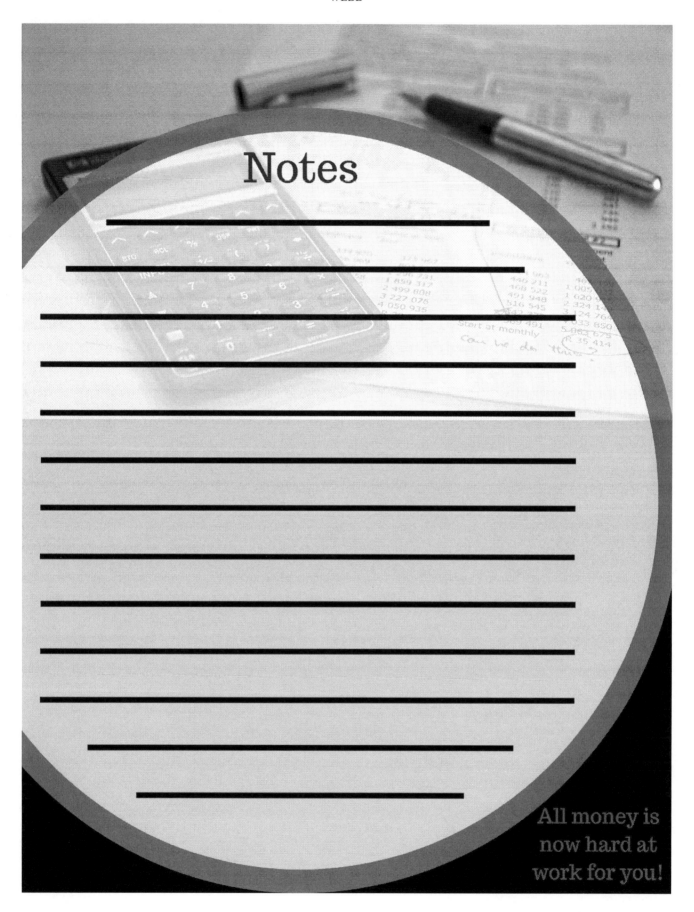

Notes

_____

_____

_____

_____

_____

_____

_____

_____

_____

_____

_____

_____

All money is now hard at work for you!

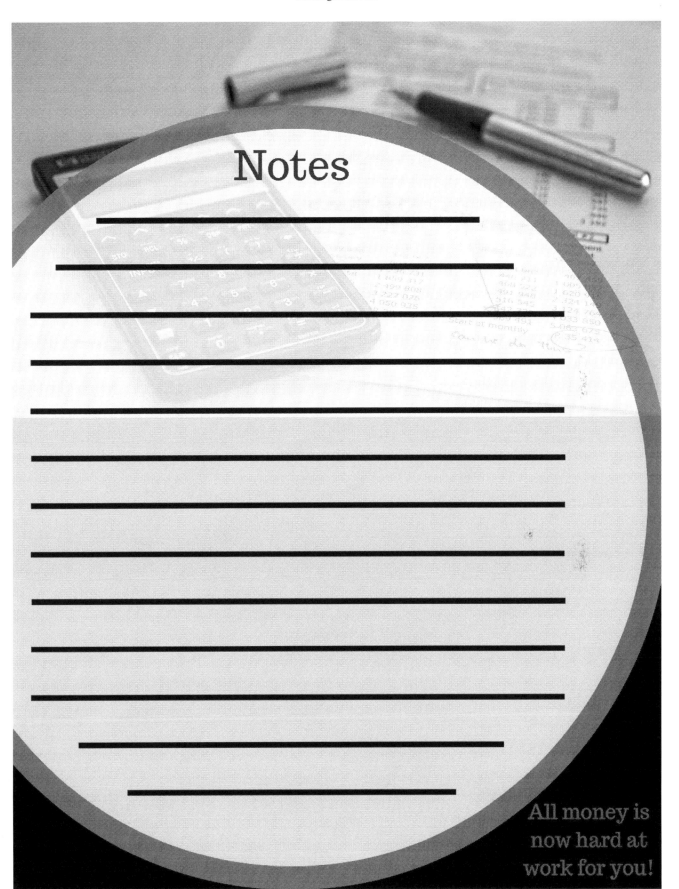

Notes

All money is
now hard at
work for you!

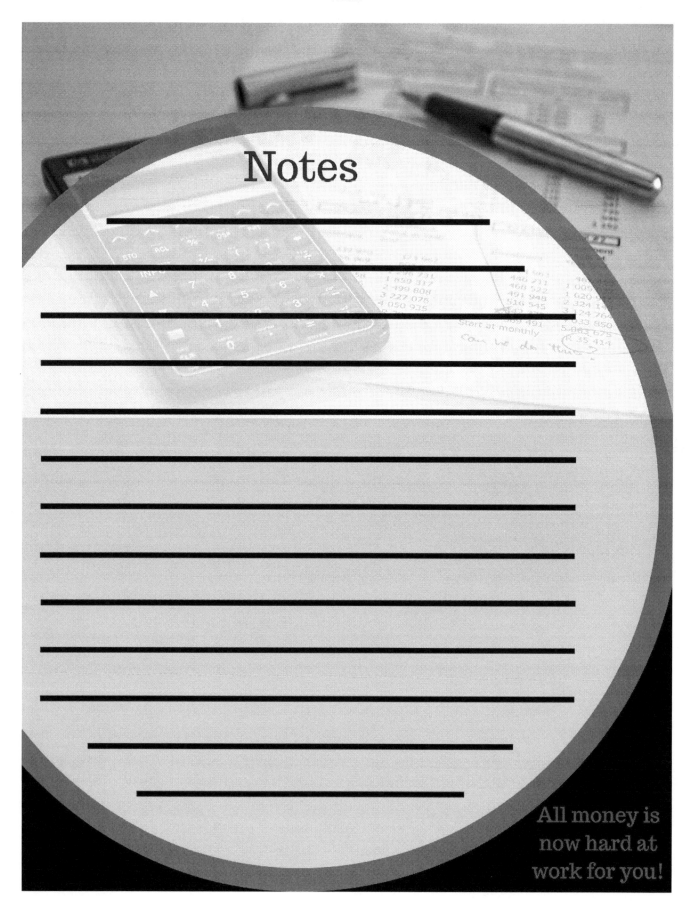

Notes

All money is now hard at work for you!

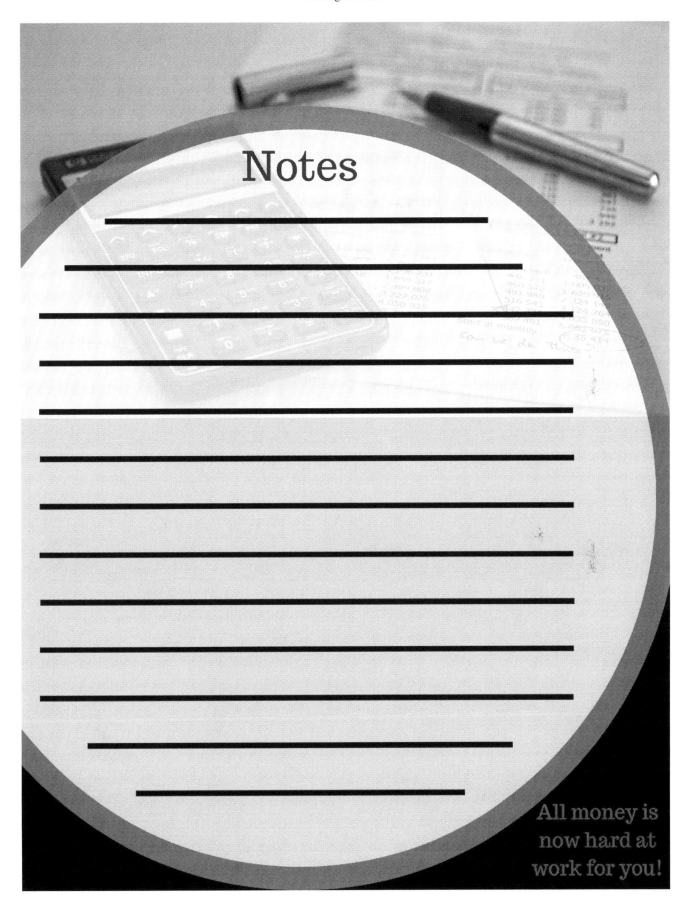

Notes

_____

_____

_____

_____

_____

_____

_____

_____

_____

_____

_____

All money is
now hard at
work for you!

Notes

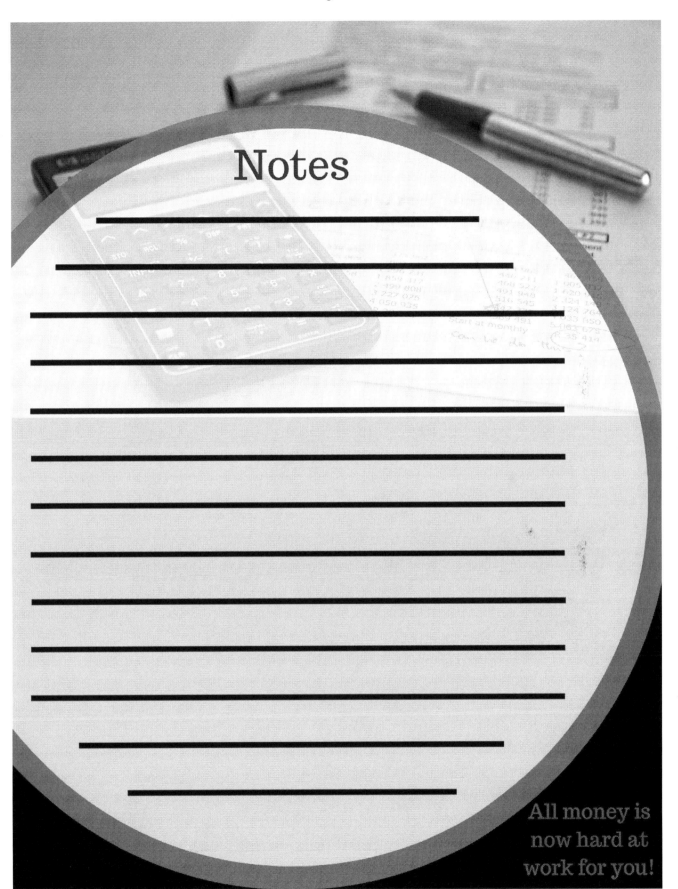

Notes

All money is
now hard at
work for you!

All money is now hard at work for you!

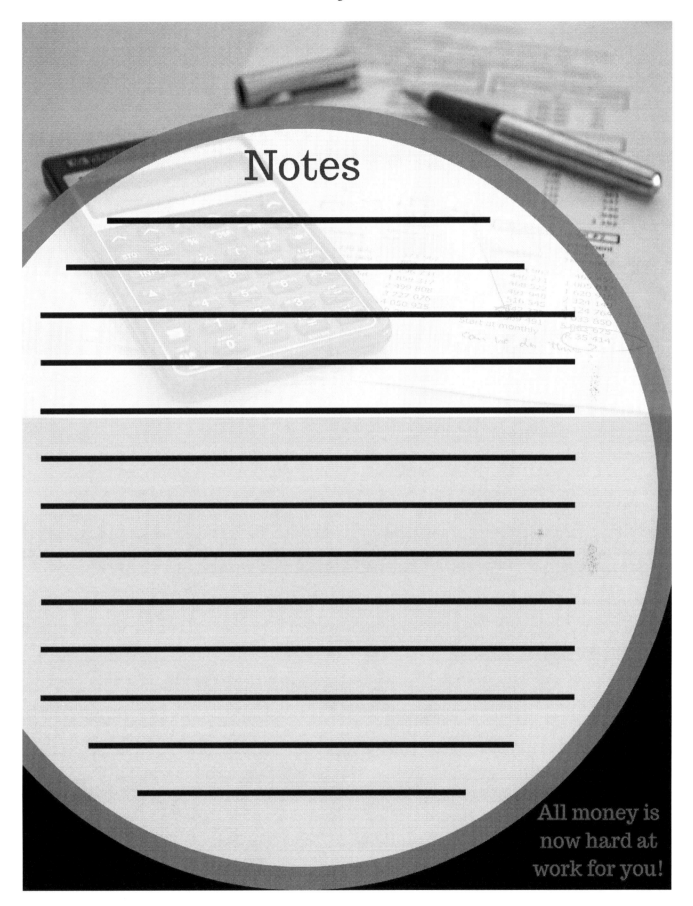

Notes

All money is now hard at work for you!

Notes

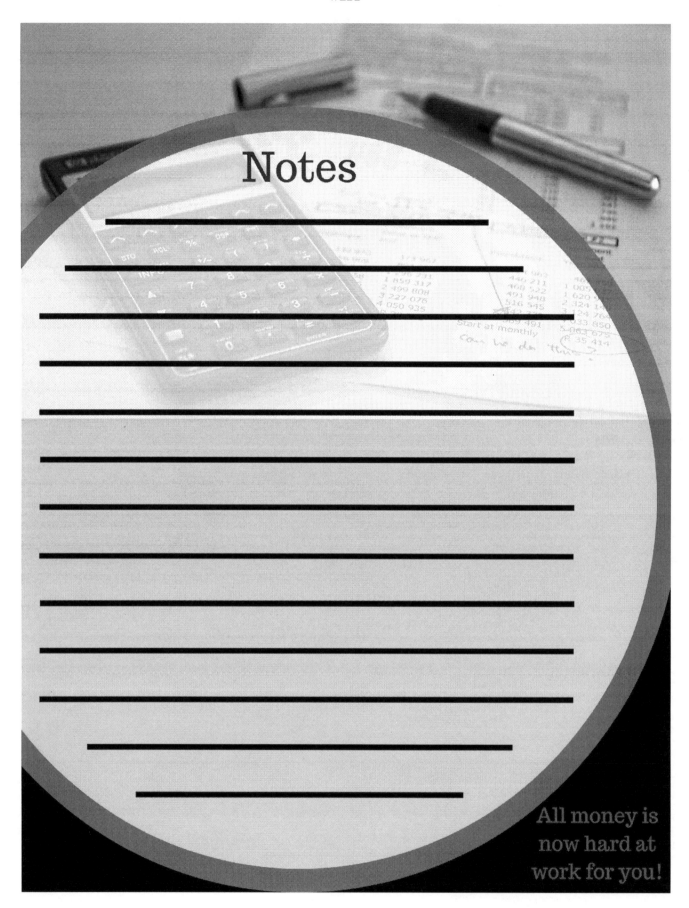

All money is now hard at work for you!

ABOUT THE AUTHOR

Rowland Webb Jr. is a former chemistry, physics, and science teacher with a Bachelor of Arts in Chemistry from the University of Virginia and Masters Degree in K-12 Physics Education from George Washington University. Upon graduation from school and early on in his career, he realized that his financial knowledge would be an important part of his plan to create wealth, financial freedom, and a solid retirement. His curiosity was peaked after noticing several differences in his retirement account growth and the growth of the S&P 500 index. Since then, Rowland has spent several years studying and learning about stocks and options. While teaching, Rowland wrote "Webb's Words of Wisdom: 10 Things Every High School Student Must Know," as a guide to assist students as they navigate through high school and on to college. He decided to focus his efforts on financial literacy because he started seeing statistics showing that the average American was one or two obstacles away from complete financial ruin. Rowland has taken several courses of study in stocks and options from organizations such as: Optionetics, ETN Trade, Options Animal, Simpler Options, and the Raging Bull group. His goal in starting TheOrdinaryInvestor.com is to empower people to participate in the stock market by learning how to invest for themselves to create wealth. He hopes that his background in teaching and experience investing will reduce the learning curve for all who participate in any workshops, seminars, or courses from TheOrdinaryInvestor.com… where we Help Ordinary Investors Create Extraordinary Wealth!

BIBLIOGRAPHY

What Is A Stock?

Team, HTMW. "What Is a Stock?" *HowTheMarketWorks Education Center*, 11 Oct. 2018, education.howthemarketworks.com/beginners/types-of-investments/stocks/intro-to-stocks/.

Voigt, Kevin, et al. "What Is Stock?" *NerdWallet*, NerdWallet, 24 Jan. 2019, www.nerdwallet.com/blog/investing/what-is-a-stock/.

"Stocks." *Investor.gov*, www.investor.gov/introduction-investing/basics/investment-products/stocks.

Engines, Financial. "Market Capitalization: Large Cap, Mid Cap & Small Cap Stocks." *Financial Engines Education Center*, 15 May 2018, financialengines.com/education-center/small-large-mid-caps-market-capitalization/.

Why Should I Invest?

Staff, US Inflation Calculator. "US Inflation Calculator." *US Inflation Calculator*, www.usinflationcalculator.com/.

"Personal Finance Statistics: How Do You Compare?" *Debt.com*, Debt.com, LLC, 11 Feb. 2019, www.debt.com/statistics/.

Reiss, Dawn. "5 Reasons to Invest in the Stock Market." *U.S. News & World Report*, U.S. News & World Report, 12 Apr. 2017, money.usnews.com/investing/articles/2017-04-12/5-reasons-to-invest-in-the-stock-market.

Staff, Motley Fool. "Why Should I Invest?" *The Motley Fool*, The Motley Fool, 16 May 2008, www.fool.com/how-to-invest/why-should-i-invest.aspx.

"Stocks." *Investor.gov*, www.investor.gov/introduction-investing/basics/investment-products/stock

"3 Reasons to Invest in Stocks." *How Mutual Funds, ETFs, and Stocks Trade - Fidelity*, 21 June 2018, www.fidelity.com/viewpoints/retirement/why-you-need-stocks.

Little, Ken. "Why You Should Invest in Stocks." *The Balance Small Business*, The Balance, 1 Feb. 2019, www.thebalance.com/part_one_the_stock_market-doesn-t-care-about-you-3141062.

"Guide to Retirement." *J.P. Morgan Institutional Asset Management*, 2018, am.jpmorgan.com/us/en/asset-management/gim/adv/insights/guide-to-retirement.

Reeves, Jeff. "Do You Know How Much You're Paying in 401(k) Fees?" *USA Today*, Gannett Satellite Information Network, 13 Jan. 2017, www.usatoday.com/story/money/personalfinance/2017/01/03/401k-fees-could-eating-away-your-retirement-savings-right-now/93819526/.

What Should I Invest In?

"Brands." *Doing What's Right | Procter & Gamble Goals and Objectives*, us.pg.com/brands/.

"Brands." *Unilever USA*, www.unileverusa.com/brands/.

"Homepage." *Content Lab - U.S.*, www.jnj.com/.

"All Sector SPDR ETFs." *Sector Tracker - Components*, www.sectorspdr.com/sectorspdr/sectors.

What About My Retirement At Work?

"Retirement Topics - Contributions." *Internal Revenue Service*, www.irs.gov/retirement-plans/plan-participant-employee/retirement-topics-contributions.

Made in the USA
Columbia, SC
26 February 2019